2009 Poetry Competition

I have a dream 2009
Words to change the world

Martin Luther King

John Lennon

Poems from Southern England
Edited by Helen Davies

First published in Great Britain in 2009 by:

Young Writers
Remus House
Coltsfoot Drive
Peterborough
PE2 9JX
Telephone: 01733 890066
Website: www.youngwriters.co.uk

All Rights Reserved
Book Design by Spencer Hart & Tim Christian
© Copyright Contributors 2009
SB ISBN 978-1-84924-491-6

Foreword

'I Have a Dream 2009' is a series of poetry collections written by 11 to 18-year-olds from schools and colleges across the UK and overseas. Pupils were invited to send us their poems using the theme 'I Have a Dream'. Selected entries range from dreams they've experienced to childhood fantasies of stardom and wealth, through to inspirational poems of their dreams for a better future and of people who have influenced and inspired their lives.

The series is a snapshot of who and what inspires, influences and enthuses young adults of today. It shows an insight into their hopes, dreams and aspirations of the future and displays how their dreams are an escape from the pressures of today's modern life. Young Writers are proud to present this anthology, which is truly inspired and sure to be an inspiration to all who read it.

Contents

Chamberlayne College for the Arts, Southampton
Heidi King (12) 1
Hannah Carr (14) 2
Jake Comley (14) 3
Joe Singleton (12) 3
Bethan Taylor (12) 4
Sophie Botting (14) 5
Jodie Maidment (11) 6
Leah Hobbs (11) 6
Kelly Kearslake (14) 7
Joshua Taggart (14) 7
Leah Jones (14) 8
Stacey Staples (12) 8
Sophie Baker (12) 9
Erin Abul (13) 9
Melissa Moody (12) 10
Sharna Sanders (12) 10
Lewis Eccleston 11
Luke Parsons (12) 11
Louise White (12) 12
Hollie Edwards (13) 12
Thomas Le Maistre (12) 13
Joe Mullett (14) 13
Sarah-Jane Hockaday (13) 14
India Bosley (12) 14
Connor Penfold (13) 15
Sarah Pearce (12) 15
Emilia Ray (11) 16
Lydia Stocker (11) 16
Katie Bambrough (13) 17
Rebecca Cole (13) 17
Christina Butcher (13) 18
Abi Miller (12) 18
Chloe D'Eath (13) 19
Alan Jones (12) 19
Samantha Boyle (13) 20
Charlotte Aldis (12) 20
Stephanie Kidd (14) 21

Fulston Manor School, Sittingbourne
Emma Hammond (12) 21
Hope Allum (12) 23
Phoebe Smith (11) 23
Joseph Hawkins (12) 25
Hannah Cooper (12) 25
Rosie Leibo (12) 27
Daniel Cale (11) 27
Danielle Woodfine (12) 28
Keziah Smith-Hassan (12) 29
Sophie Jones (11) 30
Jack Clark (11) 31
Jennifer Akhurst (12) 32
Sam Mapp (13) 33
Marita Lanceley (12) 34
Jayme Goodger (12) 35
Grace Skinner (11) 36
Jordan Pickard (12) 37
Robyn Stephenson (11) 37
Sadie Callaway (11) 38
Jack Watson (13) 38
Jennifer Hook (12) 39
Thomas Huntley (12) 39
Sam Wells (11) 40
Danny Jury (12) 40
Rachael Knowles (13) 41
Camron Philpott (11) 41
Laura-Bess Draper (11) 42
Georgia March (12) 42
Millie Davenport (12) 43
Thomas Collins (12) 43
Amber-Rose Hollands (12) 44
Billy Huntley (11) 44
Charlotte Dyke (12) 45
James Weller (11) 45
Jade Mansfield (12) 46
Brendan Johnson (11) 46
Kerry-Louise Payne (12) 47
Joshua Kisnorbo (12) 47

Jarrod White (12)	48
Zoe Moore (11)	48
Alastair Johnson-Deane (11)	49
Eve McGarry (11)	50
Charlotte Heathfield (12)	50
Jessica Vandepeer (12)	51
Ryan Croall (12)	51
Stephen Pink (12)	52
Jack Donoghue (13)	52
Bobbie Cornelius (12)	53
Stephanie Smith (13)	54
Ricky Telford (11)	55
Lilly Coward (12)	55
Tanaka Mtisi (12)	56
Ryan Mallion (12)	56
Evelyn Irwin (12)	57
Eddie Lovell (12)	57
Chris Clark (11)	58
Joseph Carlow (12)	58
Jordan Spicer (12)	59
Lauren Gridley (12)	59
Melody Butcher (13)	60
Ryan Card (11)	60
Lily Tonner (11)	61
Harley Provan (12)	61
Amy Bowling (11)	62
Aimee Pelling (12)	62
William Reynolds (12)	63
Daniel Elliott (13)	63
Jake March (12)	64
Lauren Bampton (12)	64
Katie Denny (12)	65
Shannara Harrild (12)	65
Amy Dixon (12)	66
Luke Brooks (13)	66
Alex Corden (12)	67
Joe Timmons (12)	67
Jessica Lees (13)	68
Brad Saunders (12)	68
Chloe Gillett (11)	69
Joseph Tunley (12)	69
Matthew Tumber (11)	70
Dylan Lee (13)	70
Millie Nash (11)	71
Kyah Dooley (12)	71
Beth Tumber (13)	72
Ellis Bell (13)	72
Hannah Haith (12)	73
Holly Smith (12)	74
Jordan Maddison (12)	75
Chey Caulfield (11)	75
Alice McLaughlin (12)	76
Kerri White (12)	77
Faye Davis-Smith (12)	78
Maizy Brackley (12)	79

Harris Academy, Merton
Sharmin Gafoor (12)	80
Emma-Louise Hawkins (13)	81
CJ Carrington, Sara Goddard (12), Amber, Paige, Kevin & Florence	82
Bryant Wachsmann, Joshua Yansen, O'Shane Braham & Charlie Seymour	83
Charlie Ensor	84

Heathland School, Hounslow
Saveena Mangat (14)	85
Charlotte Smith (14)	86
Dhanya Acharya (14)	87
Karisma Pankhania (14)	88

Holyport Manor School, Holyport
Daniel Compton-Williams (14)	88
Natalie Helm (15)	89
Martin Doyle (14)	90
Adam Hassani (14)	90
Lauren Way (13)	91
David Harber (15)	91
Matthew Pearson (15)	92
James McGreevy (15)	92
Usmaan Khan (15)	93
Arron Lewis (13)	94
Esther Currey (13)	95
Katy Mills (15)	95

Meadows School, Tunbridge Wells
Stephan Liennard (13)	96

Moor House School, Oxted
Luke Williams (13)	96
Elizabeth McKinnon-Green (14)	97
Paul Davordzie-Banini (14)	98

Shaid Coventon Webb (13) 99
Kane Burns (14) 99
Katrina Payne (13) 100
Caoimhe Patterson (14) 100
Romany Wixon Gibbs (14) 101

Oxted School, Oxted
Thomas Osland (12) 101
Jacob Allen (14) 102
Matt Phillips (12) 102
Brogan Smith (12) 103
William Eves (14) 103
William Gottelier (13) 104
Dominic Nolan (14) 104

Prendergast Ladywell Fields College, London
Khadija Kassim (12) 105
Shanara Bray (13) 107
Adrian Kamulegeya (11) 107
Wahida Jabarzai (13) 109
Camilla Yahaya (12) 109
Vwarhe Sodje (13) 110
Adeyemi Osundina (13) 111
Ahmed Salum (13) 112
Lizzy Dayo (13) 112
Tisharn Gordon-Josephs (12) 113
Aderinsola Adebanwo (12) 113
Pablo Bilton-Simon (12) 114
Daniel Emptage (12) 114
Rofiat Onanusi (13) 115
Andrea Teneda (13) 115
Shaun Wilson (12) 116
Robbie Lock (11) 116
Moses Dike (13) 117
Mehmet Mustafa (11) 117
Lovell McCaulay (11) 118

Rush Croft Sports College, London
Joshua Fricker (12) 118
Prince K C Numa (12) 119
Zara Nadeem 120
D'Anne Fearon (12) 121
Luke Williamson (14) 121
Hatun Soran 122

Bradley Postlethwaite (12) 122
Chris Norey 123

Salesian College, Battersea
Keanu Adorable (12) 123
Oke Omoniyi (12) 124
Dani Sherjeel (12) 125
Sam Kotovas (11) 126
Trae Johnson (11) 127
Sofiane Rincon (12) 128
Josh Clark (12) 129
Terrel Douglas (13) 130
Mack Taylor-Preston (12) 131
Jordan Dedieu (13) 131
Edward Caunca (13) 132
Moses Adewale-Duckrell (12) 132
Sean Maposa (13) 133
John Bangui (13) 133

Strathmore Centre, Twickenham
Shannon Buckthorpe 134
Connor Reddings 135
Andrea De Ville 136

The Hemel Hempstead School, Hemel Hempstead
Georgia Totten (12) 136
Charlotte Bartlett (13) 137
Amy Theobald (12) 139
Mary Pattinson (12) 141
Paige Baah (13) 141
Eliza Dickinson (12) 143
Mark Baldwin (13) 143
Ellie Ward (12) 144
Daisy 145
Grace Masters (12) 146
Jessica Miller (13) 147
George Brooks (13) 148
Francesca Quinn (12) 149
Ben Johnson (13) 150
Jodie Hardcastle (13) 151
Chris Andric (13) 152
Jade Gardiner (12) 153
Victoria Bennett (11) 154
Lauren Stone (12) 155
Kathryn Tyne (13) 156

Sophia Amamou 157
Jemma Whitbourn (12) 158
Lucy Church (11) 159
Adam Nayler (13) 160
George O'Dell (12) 161
Zoë Dennis (13) 162
Tessa Wilson (12) 163
Olivia Pinnock (12) 164
Philippa Gobby (13) 165
Charlie Hoskins (12) 166
Caitlin Filby (11) 167
Charlotte Ballard 168
Chris Mann (13) 169
Malouki Servis (14) 169
Conor Blake (13) 170
Megan McKenzie (13) 171
Christie Jackson (11) 171
Isabel & Morwenna Hooker 172
Holly Lamb (14) 172
Jordan Kelly (14) 173

Wyvern College, Laverstock
Sam Turner (13) 173
Harry Richardson (14) 174
Joshua Bartlett (14) 175
Ashley Turner (13) 176
Tom Hedges (12) 176
Taylor Budgell (13) 177
John Light (13) 178
Jacob Ashton (13) 179
Ross Keel (13) 180
Joe Willicome (12) 181
Dan Hyde (13) 182
Nick Hillier (14) 182
Scott Hutcheon (13) 183
Ben Percy (13) 183
Scott Quinn (12) 184
Ben Martin (12) 184
Harry Dredge (12) 185
Nathan Sainsbury (14) 185
Jonny Adair (12) 186
Jack Biggins (12) 186
Macauley Njie (12) 187
Dylan Hall (12) 187
Kieran Winfield (12) 188

Robert Mills (12) 188
Anthony Sturges (13) 189

The Poems

Dream

I have a dream
That is contained inside of me
I want to let it out
But I am afraid it will slip away

I have a dream
That keeps me going
Through day and night
And every day of my life

I have a dream
Inside of my bubble
It is all lonely
But wonderful at the same time

I have a dream
In my own little world
Everyone is happy
And the world is OK

I have a dream
Knocked back by reality
But I build myself up
And I come back stronger

I have a dream
Of a brighter life
Where everyone is equal
And nobody is poor

I have a dream
Of no Hell
Only Heaven
Where everyone sits on fluffy clouds

I have a dream
That will eventually come true
It is just a matter of time
Before my dream explodes to you.

Heidi King (12)
Chamberlayne College for the Arts, Southampton

I Have A Dream

I have a dream,
Four simple words,
That contain a meaning,
That could change the world.

Poverty dies,
And an ocean of tears,
Love conquers all,
Love conquers fear.

The world could be,
A place to rejoice,
With one person's help,
With one person's voice.

This person who knows,
Could even be you,
Don't give up on hope,
Don't stop being true.

We could dream the day,
Our planet becomes,
A place without violence,
A place without guns.

Or we could stop,
Think, make a stand,
Together we could change the world,
Together . . . hand in hand.

So don't just dream,
Stand out in the crowd,
Make a difference to life,
Make God be proud.

Hannah Carr (14)
Chamberlayne College for the Arts, Southampton

The Dreamer

I may be still a dreamer,
Not accomplished anything,
Pushing through the way of life,
Is becoming such a struggle,
Maybe one day I shall give up.

But I have a dream,
Will we ever get it?
Maybe not today.
Will we ever meet it?
Happiness surviving,
Through anything.

Cooking, fighting,
Could be anything.
Darkness and light,
Sleeping through,
All our dreams.

I may be still a dreamer,
Not accomplished anything,
I'm still pushing on the way,
To a greater life maybe,
One day we will succeed.

Jake Comley (14)
Chamberlayne College for the Arts, Southampton

I Have A Dream

I have a dream
It is to dream
I don't have a dream . . .
Yet.

Joe Singleton (12)
Chamberlayne College for the Arts, Southampton

Stop!

Death, war, people dying
Stop! Please stop!
This is the cry some people try to shout,
But can't be heard.
I'm starving, please feed me food . . .
Or just walk by!
Stop, please stop!
'My child is sick, we need help!'
Nearby a wealthy man walks by,
He hears but ignores.
Stop, please stop!
Guns, blood, people being shot.
'No, my baby!' a mother's cry
When her child dies in war.
Stop, please stop!
'Let the war finish . . .'
It carries on.
No one cares,
It would be better if I just died.
These thoughts go through hundreds of people's heads.
Stop, please stop!
It's too late, another innocent person dies.

Bethan Taylor (12)
Chamberlayne College for the Arts, Southampton

I Have A Dream

I have a dream
A perfect place, somewhere as cool
As outer space.
With every animal you could know,
There'll be rain and sun and snow.
Sunny beaches everywhere, for you to enjoy,
With no worries or cares.
Everyone cares, everyone's cool;
You'll have bundles of fun,
Even at school.
You will have lots of fun,
In the wind and in the sun!

In this world we live in now,
Many arguments, many rows.
Oh, how I wish they would all just stop!
Then of the world
We'd be on top.

Too many liars and cowards around,
Of music, I love the sound.
Cheers me up when I am down,
When I'm in my dressing gown.

Sophie Botting (14)
Chamberlayne College for the Arts, Southampton

Heaven's Form

I have a dream,
To be different . . .
Stronger,
Unique,
To have the power
To change the world.

Dreams are magical,
They are . . .
Hopes,
Wishes,
Desires,
Destiny.

I have a dream,
A magical dream,
To change life
And the cruel things
In it.

I have a dream . . .
Heaven in its newest form.

Jodie Maidment (11)
Chamberlayne College for the Arts, Southampton

Dreamer

I have a dream to bring,

Happiness and smiles to the world,
For families that died in the wars
And for everything people go through.

I have a dream for people
To have a happy life, with
No crime, no guns or knives . . .

Leave people alone!

Leah Hobbs (11)
Chamberlayne College for the Arts, Southampton

Believe In Your Dreams

The journey of our thoughts,
Flying through those flashing moments of existence,
Wandering footsteps leading to unplanned paths of confusion,
Falling to the force of gravity, breaking through barriers of denial.

Yet through all words spoken,
Nothing will stop me . . .
When I have a dream.

A dream that releases the soul within,
A dream that one day will be achieved through hope,
A dream where everyone can smile with pride and say,
'I'll make it too,'
A dream where everyone believes in the quality of success,
A dream where you can look into your heart saying,
'I've made it!'

I had a dream,
That came true,
Because I believed.

Kelly Kearslake (14)
Chamberlayne College for the Arts, Southampton

How Many Dreams?

How many dreams do I have?
But one by one they go.
All locked up inside my head.
I have been searching high and low
To find the key
To open the door.
What is in my dreams?
As I dive into the core,
The core of my dreams.
As I think I find it,
Or so it seems.

Joshua Taggart (14)
Chamberlayne College for the Arts, Southampton

I Have A Dream

I had a dream,
I was stood in a crowd,
All the voices were quiet,
None were out loud.

So I stood up and shouted,
Up to the sky,
'God save us!
Let poverty die!'

At once another person stood,
But with darker skin,
He raised his arms and yelled,
'Working together we win!'

All of the crowd looked up and rejoiced,
The sun shone out of the sky in choice.
The world looked up to the sky to see,
Everyone is the same as you and me!

Leah Jones (14)
Chamberlayne College for the Arts, Southampton

I Have A Dream

I magine the world calm

H aving no deaths
A nd
V ery few people gone
E veryone still there with you

A nd

D ream
R eal
E ven if
A nything
M ight not be true.

Stacey Staples (12)
Chamberlayne College for the Arts, Southampton

Dream

I have a dream,
A world of my own,
Where I am queen,
Sitting on my throne!

I have a dream,
It's burning inside,
Ready to blow,
To tell everyone!

I have a dream,
A home to see,
A family of three,
For you and for me!

I have a dream,
A hope to be revealed,
If you believe in yourself,
And you try the lead!

Sophie Baker (12)
Chamberlayne College for the Arts, Southampton

My Dream

I have a dream

H appiness will be everywhere
A ll people will live in peace
V ery calm and away from war
E veryone cares

A nd everyone shares

D ifferent coloured skin won't matter
R aces and religion won't either
E veryone is different
A ll colours, shapes and sizes
M y dream will always be a dream but it's nice to dream.

Erin Abul (13)
Chamberlayne College for the Arts, Southampton

Recipe For A Dream Coming True

1 dream
1 mixing bowl (large)
1 wooden spoon
1 raging mind
Hundreds and thousands of ideas
1 other person
1 baking tray

Preheat oven to 100°

It is recommended that you do this in the morning before breakfast.

First you get your raging mind and put it in the mixing bowl.
Next add your dream and start mixing with the wooden spoon
Until your raging mind and dream are calmed and smooth.
Put your dream into the baking tray and put into the oven for
                                                    20 minutes.
Take out and sprinkle the hundreds and thousands of ideas over.
Feed to the other person and your dream will come true.

Melissa Moody (12)
Chamberlayne College for the Arts, Southampton

I Have A Dream

I magine the world silent

H aving everything you want
A nd no one telling you what to do
V ery few arguments
E veryone working together

A nother day will come

D ay after day
R emembering all the happy thoughts
E veryone has had together
A ll day long, everyone is happy
M aybe these days will last!

Sharna Sanders (12)
Chamberlayne College for the Arts, Southampton

I Have A Dream

You may say I'm a dreamer,
That our words will never be one,
But I hope someday you'll join us,
And we can say we won.

It's really very simple,
My world will one day come true,
Whether black or white or turquoise,
My dream will be the same as you.

I have a dream that one day,
We'll be a special clan,
The world will all be friendly,
No war but peace around.

So next time you think about me,
Or your world is turned upside down,
Remember all the dreamers
And that your dreams are real.

Lewis Eccleston
Chamberlayne College for the Arts, Southampton

I Have A Dream

I   am a legend

H ow to be a legend
A top player
V alue of money
E veryone happy

A bandon the war

D ark place
R un for your life
E at healthily
A ccept money
M y poem.

Luke Parsons (12)
Chamberlayne College for the Arts, Southampton

I Have A Dream

I have a dream
That when I'm older
I want to be a millionairess
And live in Hollywood.

I have a dream
That I will be married
And have twins
A boy and a girl.

I have a dream
That I will live in a mansion
With a swimming pool
And servants.

I have a dream
That I will be famous
Go to premieres
And walk down the red carpet.

Louise White (12)
Chamberlayne College for the Arts, Southampton

I Have A Dream

I have a dream,
Where anything can happen,
Where I can fly to the highest cloud
And dive into the deepest sea,
Where magic is real
And I rule in my very own fantasy world,
Where sky-high roller coasters never end!
There's a chocolate pool
Which is always full,
Anything I want is here where I want it.
In my own world everything I do will extend
And an eternal life will never end.

Hollie Edwards (13)
Chamberlayne College for the Arts, Southampton

I Have A Dream

I have a dream
That one day there won't be hate
We will all come together to be mates

I have a dream
There won't be any fights
No guns or knives

I have a dream
That one day there won't be any racism
Because we all bleed red

Like Martin Luther King, I have a dream
That we will all be one world
Not two or three

Cos I have a dream
That we will stand tall like a tree
I have a dream.

Thomas Le Maistre (12)
Chamberlayne College for the Arts, Southampton

The Dream

I have a dream
A dream I see
I want to fly around the world
Just you and me.

I have a dream
A dream I see
We'll fly above the stars
The world will be ours.

I have a dream
A dream I see
To stroll in the universe
Just you and me.

Joe Mullett (14)
Chamberlayne College for the Arts, Southampton

I Have A Dream

I have a dream the world will be the same.
No one will be different, we'll all be whole.
I wish, I wish for there to be no evil or sickness.
I have a dream, I have a dream.
Speaking words to change the world.
Bang! Crash! Another person is in danger.
Oh, how I wish, oh, how I wish.
One voice on the stand,
There goes another evil town.
I have a dream, I have a dream.
No one goes without food or clothes.
Water for all, houses for all.
Oh, I wish, oh, I wish.
The world will be the same,
The world will be a nicer place.

Sarah-Jane Hockaday (13)
Chamberlayne College for the Arts, Southampton

Dreams

When I lay in bed at night,
I close my eyes real tight,
I pull the duvet over me
And this is what I see . . .

Soft black bunnies
Chewing on moist, green grass,
White horses riding the waves,
Fluffy clouds floating through the sky,
The sun beating down warm upon my face.

When I lay in bed at night,
I close my eyes real tight.
I think of everything I can be,
Guess I'll have to wait and see!

India Bosley (12)
Chamberlayne College for the Arts, Southampton

Imagine

I magine

H aving a dream
A dream that inspires change, inspires a generation of peace
V acations away from war
E qualities throughout the world

A ctions speaking louder than words

D ream of this world
R emaking broken civilisations
E ager to change
A voice in the crowd
M aking a difference.

   Imagine.

Connor Penfold (13)
Chamberlayne College for the Arts, Southampton

I Have A Dream

I have a dream

H ow to bring happiness to the world
A life where there is no fighting
V ery few arguments
E very dream counts

A mbitions are people's dreams

D reams are people's ambitions
R ather many people persevere
E very single person counts
A nybody counts
M y dream will be reality
   And so will yours!

Sarah Pearce (12)
Chamberlayne College for the Arts, Southampton

Dreams - An Opportunity

Dreams have a magic touch
That you can't help fall for.
It could be to change the world
Or just plain fantasy.

The decision is yours
Whether or not you take it
It's there forever
You just have to reach out.

The option is in front of you
But you choose to ignore it
What becomes of the world then?
An opportunity wasted.

Emilia Ray (11)
Chamberlayne College for the Arts, Southampton

Dreaming

People always dream
Of the things that they love.
Their ambitions, hopes and dreams,
That they want to come true.

Travelling the world, or being a sports star,
Or just having fun, that's what they want.
Some people want a quiet life,
And some want to go far.

People have different dreams,
That's what dreaming's about.
Following your dreams could change your life,
But leave them alone and they will stay dreams.

Lydia Stocker (11)
Chamberlayne College for the Arts, Southampton

I Have A Dream

A mystery in the darkness,
An adventure in the day,
Hidden beneath the surface,
Is where the secrets lay.

Just wish upon a shooting star,
A dream that will come true,
A perfect happy ending,
Is destined for me and you.

Belief, fate, love and hope,
The world is not what it seems,
Be true to yourself forever,
I had a dream.

Katie Bambrough (13)
Chamberlayne College for the Arts, Southampton

I Have A Dream

I have a dream
To own Primark
Where I'm the boss
And they listen to me

To run around each night
And try things on
Running up the escalators
And running all the way back down

To go to the till
And realise I don't have to pay
And to tell everyone that . . .
The shop's all mine!

Rebecca Cole (13)
Chamberlayne College for the Arts, Southampton

I Have A Dream

I have a dream of becoming a hairdresser,
Cutting the hair of the models
Like Kate Moss and Keira Knightley.

I have a dream of becoming a singer,
Will it happen or not?
Going on tours and meeting other bands,
But becoming rich and famous.

At the moment they seem too far away,
I'm getting there, step by step.
Will it happen? I don't know . . .
I have a dream.

Christina Butcher (13)
Chamberlayne College for the Arts, Southampton

My Dream

When I go to bed tonight,
I know what I'll see,
My dream,
My dream.

My dream is to start a new world,
One where life feels new,
Where poor people live as middle class do,
A world where happiness is contagious.

Imagine this being real,
Your babies being born into a world of peace,
Imagine - that is my dream.

Abi Miller (12)
Chamberlayne College for the Arts, Southampton

I Have A Dream

Dreams are all about hope
Everyone has dreams.

My dream is to dance,
To spin and twirl all over the world.

To work alongside singers
And other dancers doing what I love.

With thousands of people coming to watch me
While I dance all over the stage!

Dreams are all about hope
And what you do with your life.

Chloe D'Eath (13)
Chamberlayne College for the Arts, Southampton

Piano Player

The piano is a marvellous thing,
Where you play and play to make a tune,
As the notes fill up in your head.

People come from miles on end,
To see your own lovely masterpiece,
With each note played, the more they cheer.

Your inspiration is anything you desire,
And all of your loved ones,
So now you know, go and compose your own piece.

Alan Jones (12)
Chamberlayne College for the Arts, Southampton

Dream!

D ark and scary dreams can be, but also peaceful in your own fantasy
R ed, white or green, anything can happen with family or friends, anything can be
E verything is real, you can fly, sing in front of millions or be the queen
A dventures, love lost then found, wealth, the most in the world
M onsters in the dark, wedding of your dreams comes true, dream your own little place of fantasy.

Samantha Boyle (13)
Chamberlayne College for the Arts, Southampton

Dreaming

D is for doodles
R is for reality
E is for exciting
A is for ambitious
M is for memories
I is for imagination
N is for nightmares
G is for generous.

Charlotte Aldis (12)
Chamberlayne College for the Arts, Southampton

I Have A Dream

I have a dream
That the people in poverty get help
That animals in pain don't have to yelp
That third world countries get the food they need
That the homeless people get money to feed
That the people in Africa get their drink
And if we all get together and think
These dreams can become reality.

Stephanie Kidd (14)
Chamberlayne College for the Arts, Southampton

I Have A Dream

I have a dream to one day be an actress
To be in a film or to star as a princess
I have a dream that one day I'll go diving
Or go gliding in the air, wow I'll be flying!

I have a dream that the war will finally stop
And for peace to start again, right from the top
I have a dream for poverty to end
So every child and adult will be on the mend.

I have a dream to travel the world
On a boat, on a plane, I'll be a famous little girl
I have a dream that the money is mine to own
And that I'll be rich, then I'll never moan!

I have a dream I'll be a hairdresser
Then be recommended for a fashion designer
I have a dream to be in the Olympics
To show off my gymnastics, with fabulous flips.

I have a dream that I'll reach all these wonders
Even if it rains, even if it thunders
For although my dreams can be hard to do
The only thing really stopping yourself is you.

Emma Hammond (12)
Fulston Manor School, Sittingbourne

I Have A Dream

Believe
You could be whatever you want
Believe
That you could be a rock star
Believe
You could be in the Olympics
Believe
You could be a model
Believe
That you had ten wishes
Believe
You can have anything you want
Believe
You could be invisible
Believe
You could control the world
Believe
You could go back in time
Believe
That you stopped all the world wars
Believe
You made bullying stop
Believe
That you had the dream phone that you have always wanted
Believe
That you could move anything with the click of a finger
Believe
You were magic
Believe
You were the world's prettiest and most handsome person
In the world
Believe
You made the world a better place
Believe
You are rich
Believe
You lived in a mansion
Believe
You lived on the moon

Believe
You could control the other people
Believe
You lived in Paris
Believe
You were Italian
Believe
You were the fastest person ever born
Believe
You can change age whenever and wherever you want
Believe
That you can never die
Believe
You could be reborn
Believe
You could do whatever you wanted and not get told off for it
Just believe
In yourself.

Hope Allum (12)
Fulston Manor School, Sittingbourne

I Have A Dream

I have a dream,
The cattle roam,
To be once more,
On the shore.
I have a dream,
We all get along,
There is no war,
In the world.
I have a dream,
That our world is lovely.
I have a dream,
The grass is green,
The water flows,
So we call Earth home.

Phoebe Smith (11)
Fulston Manor School, Sittingbourne

Dreams Of The Future

The future is as unclear
As the dirtiest waters
And as unpredictable
As the mind of a baby

The dreams of the future
Vary depending on the character
The position and the situation,
The lonely man who is madly in love
Dreams of his wedding
The most beautiful girl in a white dress
A graceful, white swan, as pure as the Virgin Mary
The future brings many things

The worried mother dreams of the war ending
Her son returning home
No more deadly bullets flying through the burning, screaming air
No more friends dead
Hateful thoughts running through his mind
The future brings many things

The lone outsider dreams of being accepted
No matter what religion
Colour of skin
Class, shape or size
To not fear stabbing and shooting
To not be stared at by the neighbourhood gang
The future brings so many things

I hope to see a new world
New people and places
To die in a better place
Peacefully, gracefully
I hope the creatures will be treated well

Like a brother or sister
The future holds many fears
The future brings many things
Both amazing and beautiful
Or tragic and tearful.

Joseph Hawkins (12)
Fulston Manor School, Sittingbourne

With The Right Words

With the right words I can change people's minds
About what they say and do.
Life could be easy if we listen to the cries of others
Screaming for help, instead of people ignoring them.
The world having no fear of humanity's differences and addictions.
We could live in peace and harmony
If we think about what we say and do.

With the right words they can stand in the light
And feel the pure rain on their burning skin.
With life in the shadows, hope will always bring bright,
                                      burning candles,
Leading the way to happiness and joy.
The world could be different
If others were not selfish and demanding.
Sorrow hangs over the ones without homes, money, families . . . lives.
Their soft cries whistle through the air,
Their spindly arms cling to each other, no parents to comfort them.
We can stop war and misfortune if they stand in the light.

With the right words we could save the Earth.
Working together to crush the plans of man-made mistakes.
We could stop wars which last for eternity.
We should always remember smiles instead of grudges we've had,
We are Earth's defenders? Destroyers? Savers?
Think of the world before ourselves, as without the world there
                                                        is no us.
We could save the Earth with the right words.

Hannah Cooper (12)
Fulston Manor School, Sittingbourne

My Birthday Dream

When it's my birthday,
I have a dream,
Are you wondering?
Let's hear the theme.
It would be a big disco,
With all my friends,
We will be dancing,
Until it's the end
And no, I'm not talking about
The end of the day,
No, no, no, no, no, no,
No way.
I'm talking about the end of
The year,
Wahay!
The food would be junk food
And the pudding,
Yes please!
This would be the best birthday,
Mum plans just for me.
Who was there?
I'll list them for you,
There is more than one
And there is more than two,
There is Gemma and Katie,
Paige, Jayme,
Yes!
This is my party
And yes, it's the best!
All of my presents,
Are the best of all time,
I open them whilst Mum
Is drinking wine.
I get a laptop,
Some make-up,
Some new luminous things
And from Nanny I get
Some fabulous bling-bling!

So now I repeat,
Oh yes, yes, yes,
This is my birthday
And yes, it's the best!

Rosie Leibo (12)
Fulston Manor School, Sittingbourne

Weather

Wet and raining in the day,
Miserable places and also misery on people's faces.
People walk by, they say,
'Why can't there be rain in Bombay?'

Wet and raining in the day,
Nowhere to play.
Children playing in the rain,
Mums and dads trying to get them out of the wet.

The wet, cold wind whistling on your face,
Frosting your entire face, forehead to chin.
You look outside
And see the sky's faded to grey.

The weather is changing,
There's no one out there,
No animals, no birds singing to each other,
Nothing, nothing is out there.

It's so cold there, snow lying on the ground,
But the sun is peering out of the clouds.
It's night-time, but the sunlight is so bright at night, shining.
The stars reflect the light,
Making the night sky as bright as possible,
The snow is melting fast, spring is on its way to play.

Spring loves to play on a wet day,
The sun is out, the sky is blue,
This is my best day,
How about you?

Daniel Cale (11)
Fulston Manor School, Sittingbourne

I Have A Dream

My dreams are very special to me
And I would like for them to come true
But sometimes you have to wait and wait
Until the waiting time is through.

I would love to stop racism
It's the one thing I would do
But when it's one against thousands
It's hard trying not to lose.

Singing and dancing, designing and hairdressing
That is what I'd want to achieve
So I have to work hard in life
And then I can start to believe.

Long, short, layered, straight
All the kinds of hair
But the one thing I would love to do
Is chop it so it's bare.

Music, mikes, speakers, stage
That's how I'd love to be
A singer with an assistant and stuff
And it all revolves around me!

Dancing, turning, plies and twists
That's my dream too
But nothing can be more special
For me to do.

Skirts, tops, shoes and shorts
The clothes that I love the best
So when I get older
I won't need a fashion test.

They're my dreams and ambitions
And I hope they all come true!

Danielle Woodfine (12)
Fulston Manor School, Sittingbourne

I Have A Dream

I have a dream, it's life,
And becoming something successful in it,
Dream whatever you want to dream,
It's one life,
And it's too short,
Go for it,
Be what you want to be,
And go for it,
Do whatever,
Go for it,
Do it,
I have always wanted to be as successful as him (Grandad),
He inspired me,
I will follow what he taught me,
Told me and went on about it,
Went on and on,
Getting carried away,
But I know he just wants to help.
And her (Nan),
Always getting me what I want,
Just wants to please me,
Never wants to see me unhappy,
It would kill
Last of all her (Mum),
She wants me to do so well in life,
Always helping me with homework,
Wants me to go for it,
It's life, it's too short to let it fly by,
I love you, Mum.
Then I come back to my dream,
I had a dream.

Keziah Smith-Hassan (12)
Fulston Manor School, Sittingbourne

Grandad

I have a dream,
A wish of love,
To love someone,
From above,
My grandad,
I wish to see,
To smell, to feel,
To know for real,
To see what you look like,
What you sound like,
I only have memories from my dad,
Thinking about it makes me sad.
The trees sway, when I pray and pray,
For my dream to come true,
I wish I could see you.
My dad said you had
A great smile and lots of hair,
To not see you I can't bear,
You liked sports and you loved cats.
My dream is a puzzle with a missing piece,
The picture is of you giving me a cuddle,
Oh, please fill this puzzle.
People ask me, 'Have you had a good day?'
I say, 'Yes.' Deep down no is the answer
As you are not there to say
'I love you'. Please, saying 'I love you' will fill my heart.
I have a dream,
A wish of love,
To love someone
From above . . .
I love you, Grandad.

Sophie Jones (11)
Fulston Manor School, Sittingbourne

I'd Like To See A World

The Earth is just one world,
Why do you choose to destroy it?
I'd like to see a world,
Where everyone can enjoy it.

We switch on the TV,
And see it all first hand,
I'd like to see a world,
Where we're not fighting over land.

A trip into the city,
Shouldn't mean the end of life,
I'd like to see a world,
Where it's safe to be alive.

Thousands of innocent victims,
A building and a plane,
I'd like to see a world,
Where we won't see that again.

Attacking and slaying,
With bombs and guns and mines,
I'd like to see a world,
Where we all have happier times.

Clean water and good food,
For the starving and weak,
I'd like to see a world,
Where everyone gets to eat.

The end of cruel dictators,
Filled with power and greed,
I'd like to see a world,
That brings destruction to its knees.

Jack Clark (11)
Fulston Manor School, Sittingbourne

My Dream

A little kitten in a box, shivering out in the rain.
Why?
A loyal dog by the door, whimpering for you to come home.
Why?
A beaten bear made to dance for a street sideshow.
Why?
I have a dream
To stop cruelty to animals.
All animals, great and small,
From fine, fat and furry
To shabby, skinny and scaly.

Animals' feelings are the same as ours,
So why should we treat them any differently?
Why can't we live in a world
Where a dog is a man's best friend,
Not a punch bag?
Where a bear is strong and mighty,
Not weak and scared?

Animals are loyal to their owners
And stay with them through thick and thin.
Yet we are not loyal back,
Instead we abandon them,
Starving in an empty house.
Freezing out in the darkening park,
Beaten, chained and humiliated.

Animals can't stand up for themselves,
Unlike me or you.
Humans are treated with love and respect,
And animals should be too.

Jennifer Akhurst (12)
Fulston Manor School, Sittingbourne

I Have A Dream

I have a dream

Where everyone can appreciate what they have,
Not to go and buy something
Only to waste it.

I have a dream

Look at the people in Africa,
Who would love to get an education,
You have an education,
But you don't want to learn.

I have a dream

There are people in Africa
Who walk three miles for water,
But some of us just take the mick
By leaving the tap on when we don't need it.

I have a dream

Don't take for granted what you have,
The next time you leave the tap on,
Remember what the people in Africa
Would do for a clean glass of water.

And for those who refuse to learn,
Just be lucky,
Because if you think about those who don't
You might just realise,
How lucky you are.

Sam Mapp (13)
Fulston Manor School, Sittingbourne

Let Us Stop It!

A silent graveyard except for the mourning wind,
Thousands of crosses,
With no names to remember,
Those who died for war,
Let us stop it!

The snow comes; a silent ghost waiting to be found,
No one visits,
Spring comes; a spark of life amongst eternal rest,
No one visits,
Summer, autumn and snow once more,
So many lost souls, never to be remembered,
Let us stop it!

It has been five years since my father's fall,
I awaken in the night, like a baby yearning for love,
Shouting out: 'Father, please come back to me!'
Searching, wanting, hoping he is with me,
But all I hear is the whispering of the curtains,
Let us stop it!

All Mother does is shed tears of grief,
Her face showing the pain of loss; a soul deprived of love,
I wish I could give her words of comfort and reassurance,
That he still lives within us, a long-lost beat,
But I have to make my way,
To try and stop the misery,
I will stop it!

Marita Lanceley (12)
Fulston Manor School, Sittingbourne

Maybe The Army's Not For Me

I sat and announced to Mum,
'I'm going to be in the army!'
She turned around and said,
'A girl like you? You must be barmy!'

They were sitting,
Polishing their boots with great care,
I could not decide
What lipgloss to wear.

Everyone stayed still,
Trying to concentrate,
Until I asked my mate
If my hair was still straight.

We were on the front line,
Waiting to fire,
While I was sitting there,
With my nails under the dryer!

It was all quiet,
We were trying to sleep,
When my boyfriend texted me
With a loud bleep.

Maybe my mum was right,
The army's not for me.
I will find another career,
Who knows what it will be?

Jayme Goodger (12)
Fulston Manor School, Sittingbourne

I Have A Dream

I have a dream
That one day I'll be,
Flying across the sky,
With my hands held up high,
Waving goodbye.

I have a dream
That some day you'll see,
The world in a nicer way,
Give money to the poor,
Buy food for the hungry,
We'll stop fighting one day.

I have a dream
The world would seem,
Different in every way,
No wars, knife crime or gun crime.

I have a dream
That some day we'll see,
Ethnic people as they really are,
Let's not judge them by the colour of their skin.

I have a dream
That one day,
The world will be
A better place for us to live in,
A place where all the family can have fun.

Grace Skinner (11)
Fulston Manor School, Sittingbourne

I Have A Dream

My goal is to go to the top of the sky and rest with
The people that God has chosen to relax with Him
And His angels.
He will carefully pick the good and
Bad so the people in the future can finally meet
Their ancestors.
My goal is to go under the ocean
And swim just above the seabed to watch the
Other fish get on with their perfect lives not
Worrying about anything.
My goal is to see what is
Under lava and to find out what bugs and other
Animals live and eat under the surface.
For all I know
There might not even be anything under
There at all.
My goal is to run in the flowers to my
True love and lay down with a picnic and no
Distractions.
My goal is to climb a mountain with
All my best friends and know that I did something
Good
And know that my friends will help if I fall.

Jordan Pickard (12)
Fulston Manor School, Sittingbourne

I Dream Of Egypt

I dream about all the things I could do
When I go to Egypt, like:

Swimming in the Dead Sea and seeing all the coral reefs,
I dream I could climb a pyramid and go sunbathing,
But there's so much I want to see and do in this different land,
But to make this happen I have a plan . . .

Robyn Stephenson (11)
Fulston Manor School, Sittingbourne

I Have A Dream

I have a dream that I'm on holiday
In Hawaii for a day
Lying on the beach with the sun in the sky
As I watch the time pass by
The palm trees sway side to side
When the wind can't decide
Just a day, a week will do
I'll be glad for company too
I haven't had the change to go there before
But if I do I would like to go on a tour
To see the palm trees and get a tan
And to see the golden, warm sand
Also I would go in the sea
Then after I would go for my tea
I watch the stars every night
As I hope for that one tonight
For the one that will take me there
Just take me there, please, tonight
My shooting star, shining bright
It's the shooting star, what else will it be?
I just hope it comes to me
The greatest star in the world that makes your dreams come true
Hawaii, this wish is for you.

Sadie Callaway (11)
Fulston Manor School, Sittingbourne

I Had A Dream

If I had a dream everything would be made of ice cream
If I had a dream I would run like a running bean
If I had a dream everything would be green - but it will never be seen
If I had a dream I would be lean not mean
If I had a dream everything would be made of ice cream

Wouldn't that be your dream?

Jack Watson (13)
Fulston Manor School, Sittingbourne

I Have A Dream

I have a dream that I hope will come true some day
But all I can do at the moment is sit here and pray.

I have a dream to do hair and beauty
To cut a few hairstyles and buff up some nails
Please let me have this dream.

I have a dream to travel the world
See all the amazing sights and try all the different foods.

I have a dream that I can have a brother or sister
That I can play with when they are bored
And say that I am not an only child.

I have a dream to have a fantastic singing voice
To wow the crowd like my friend does.

I have a dream to be like my mum
To have a successful business and work as hard as I can.

I have a dream to be a famous horse rider
To win a few medals
So everyone knows what a good sportsman I am.

Please let me have my dreams
Please let them happen
But all I do at the moment is sit there and imagine . . .

Jennifer Hook (12)
Fulston Manor School, Sittingbourne

I Have A Dream

When I close my eyes
What I see is the whole world before me
As the greatest scientist of all time
I love it all, it is very cool
Beakers, Bunsen burners and chemicals too
Fill me with joy, how about you?

Thomas Huntley (12)
Fulston Manor School, Sittingbourne

I Had A Dream

I had a dream
Let's hope it comes true
I'd like to be a sculptor
Through and through

I wish I was not allergic
So I could have a dog
But this is just a dream I feel
That can't come true
It must be just a fog

I wish there was new technology
I'd be over the moon
Let's hope this will happen
Very, very soon

Why do we have homework?
We already spend the day
Listening to the teacher
Who always has her say

I always dream of home
It is a time to rest
But given all this homework
I hope it's not a test . . .

Sam Wells (11)
Fulston Manor School, Sittingbourne

I Have A Dream

Imagine if you smoke
At the age of 12 you make that bloke
Get that last pack off the shelf
You will have bad health
And it would all be on you
And you'd steal money to calm your craving
Gatecrashing parties and going out raving.

Danny Jury (12)
Fulston Manor School, Sittingbourne

My Nan

I admire my nan,
She is always there for me,
Snuggle on the sofa,
Play and plait my hair,
I love my nan.

She makes me laugh all the time,
When she's had a glass of wine,
She's the entertainment of the party,
I love my nan.

Even when the sky is grey
And it's pouring down with rain,
She is there dancing
With a massive smile on her face.
When she has bad news,
She has a shoulder to cry on
And will be there for you.
I love my nan.

I would like to say
Thank you Nan for everything
You have done for me.
I love you.

Rachael Knowles (13)
Fulston Manor School, Sittingbourne

Above The Stars

I have a dream, I wish that:
I could fly above the moon,
Above the moon, above the stars,
Or even above the Milky Way.
I know that this is an impossible dream,
But it still counts as a dream
And a beautiful one too!

Camron Philpott (11)
Fulston Manor School, Sittingbourne

I Have A Dream

I have a dream,
To help young children
Live their lives in a
Happy way . . .

I have a dream,
To stop the suffering
Of children who have to
Put up with abuse . . .

I have a dream,
To unlock the door
And set free what's
Inside . . .

I have a dream,
To make others' dreams
Come true . . .

I have a dream,
To keep children safe
Until help comes . . .

I have a dream,
To be a social worker!

Laura-Bess Draper (11)
Fulston Manor School, Sittingbourne

My Dream

My dream is like no other.
My dream is helpful and kind.
My dream is fair.
My dream is to live in Africa
And help comfort, feed and care for the children there.
My dream can be done.
My dream can only be done if you help me.

Georgia March (12)
Fulston Manor School, Sittingbourne

I Have A Dream

I have a dream,
To change the world,
I have a dream,
To have world peace,
I have a dream,
No wars, no army,
I have a dream,
No hurt or pain,
I have a dream,
No fights, no blood,
I have a dream,
To make a difference,
I have a dream,
Me up there,
I have a dream,
To know everyone,
I have a dream,
No hunger, no suffering,
I have a dream,
No arguments,
I have a dream,
To be happy!

Millie Davenport (12)
Fulston Manor School, Sittingbourne

My Dream

I have a dream to bring peace to the world
I have a dream to make everyone heard
I have a dream to stop racism in every corner of the world
I have a dream to live a good life without trouble or strife
I have a dream
Some dreams do come true.

Thomas Collins (12)
Fulston Manor School, Sittingbourne

Global Warming

I had a dream,
That global warming stopped,
That the pollution had gone
And the world was a cleaner place.

I had a dream,
That global warming stopped,
There was no harm
And all the animals were calm.

I had a dream,
That global warming stopped,
Where the skies were vivid blue
And the world looked new.

I had a dream,
That global warming stopped,
The air smelt fresh
And the streams tasted so sweet.

I had a dream,
That global warming stopped,
The world was such a magnificent place
And everybody was safe.

Amber-Rose Hollands (12)
Fulston Manor School, Sittingbourne

Dreams And Ambition

I have the same dream all the time,
The whole world's riches will be mine.
To have fifteen houses in the country,
With wallpaper made out of money.
The hounds will protect my honey,
That is how I made my money.
I have a helicopter to make my escape,
To the island of the great.

Billy Huntley (11)
Fulston Manor School, Sittingbourne

A Dream Is A Dream

Acting. On stage, one million miles away from reality.
Writing. Half dead yet still running for your life or perhaps a
romantic love story.
The dream is yours, no matter what you choose.

Running. For the Olympics or just for fun.
Stardom. Singing your heart out to those that love you,
or maybe kicking a football around on TV.
Your dream is something only you can decide on.

Painting. Something worthy to be admired or is it just to say
thanks to a friend?
Creating a scene. You're a photographer putting together something
you might be awarded for or rather a film director making
everything perfect.
What is a dream?

An astronaut. In your spaceship with no gravity or is it that you
wanted to steer the ship?
A family. Looking after a special someone you love and maybe
running outside with the kids.
I suppose a dream really is a dream . . .

What a crazy thought that was!

Charlotte Dyke (12)
Fulston Manor School, Sittingbourne

I Have A Dream

I have a dream that I can play cricket for England
I have a dream that I could go to Mars
I have a dream that I could eat nothing but chocolate bars
I have a dream that I could fly
I have a dream that I could never die
I have a dream to rule the world
I have a dream to do everything
I will only rest when it's all done!

James Weller (11)
Fulston Manor School, Sittingbourne

Imagine

Imagine
I could be a singer
When I am older

Imagine
I could be a pianist
When I am older

Imagine
I could be a linguist
When I learn more languages

Imagine
I could be an artist
When I learn more

Imagine
I could be a person
Who works with children

I admire my sisters
I admire my brothers
But I also admire my cousins

I wish I could be all these.

Jade Mansfield (12)
Fulston Manor School, Sittingbourne

I Have A Dream

I have a dream to make people better
I have a dream to change the weather
I have a dream to change the world
Dreams that make a big difference
I have a dream to cure cancer
I have a dream to be an Irish dancer
I have a dream to change the world
Dreams that make a big difference.

Brendan Johnson (11)
Fulston Manor School, Sittingbourne

I Have A Dream

I have a dream,
Burning up inside me,
Like a fire burning away,
One day I will see,
This dream is made for me.

I have a dream,
Our fantasy,
A wondrous ride,
For you and I,
We can all be happy.

I have a dream,
Light shining upon me,
Like a candle in the night,
Now I see,
Dreams are meant for everyone.

I have a dream,
Now I see,
We can be
In our own fantasy,
This dream is right for me.

Kerry-Louise Payne (12)
Fulston Manor School, Sittingbourne

TTT

Smoking isn't clever, it will kill you you know,
Bullying needs to stop, you need to tell someone to let it show,
Drugs equals addiction, if you carry on you will end up fiction,
Hoodies need to stop and look at what they have done,
Depression - you should walk with your head up and don't let anyone
                                        put you down.

My perfect world would be:
Termination of teenage terror.

Joshua Kisnorbo (12)
Fulston Manor School, Sittingbourne

Pro BMXer Poem

I dream I'd like to be a
Pro BMXer when I'm older,
Flying through the air
And doing tricks everywhere,
Riding round without a care.

I dream I'd like to be a
Pro BMXer when I'm older,
Barspin way up high,
Reaching for the sky,
Feeling the wind rushing by.

I dream I'd like to be a
Pro BMXer when I'm older,
Tail whip to flair,
'X up' in the air,
Triple backflip if I dare.

I dream I'd like to be a
Pro BMXer when I'm older,
Getting a sponsorship deal,
Winning my first trophy,
Maybe a thrill.

Jarrod White (12)
Fulston Manor School, Sittingbourne

Dreams

Dreams are what you want out of life,
Dreams are things that float in your mind,
A dream is the butterfly in your heart,
And soon that butterfly will fly out of your heart and into the open,
But that will only happen if you believe in that dream!

Zoe Moore (11)
Fulston Manor School, Sittingbourne

My Dream

If I had a dream, just one dream,
It would surely be to fly like a bird,
With the wind in my face.
I would fly around the world
To see France and Spain
And even Germany.
That would surely be my dream
As my wings would be like a pillow
That I could snuggle up to night after night.
I would peer into people's gardens,
Looking for something to eat,
I would try to stay clear
Of all those restless cats,
As they don't seem to like things with wings.
I think I would love it,
As there is a lot to see.
Things like mountains and grass so green,
Oceans and icebergs, deserts and forests.
The whole world beneath my wings.
I think I would love it.
Wouldn't you?

Alastair Johnson-Deane (11)
Fulston Manor School, Sittingbourne

I Dream

I dream I could fly
I dream I could be famous
I dream it could be sunny every day
I dream

I dream I could be a cat
So I could sleep all day
I dream that I could have happy dreams
I dream the most random things
I dream

I dream that people are all kind
I dream that the summer holidays last forever
I dream that there are creatures beyond the imaginary
I dream

I dream that dreams aren't real
I dream that I will never fly
I dream that the summer holidays
Won't last forever
I dream that all people are kind
I dream.

Eve McGarry (11)
Fulston Manor School, Sittingbourne

This Is My Dream!

My dream, my dream,
My sweet, sweet dream,
To sing and dance,
To laugh and prance.

To play around,
Not make a sound,
To play all day,
And at the end say . . .
'Yay!'

Charlotte Heathfield (12)
Fulston Manor School, Sittingbourne

I Have A Dream

I have a dream to drift away,
With all the clouds
On a sunny day.

I have a dream to dance and sing,
I love the soft notes
Of a violin.

I have a dream to have a laugh
And one day go down
The red carpet path.

I have a dream to jump and scream,
Jumping makes me sweat
So I lick ice cream.

I have a dream, a dream to fly,
To stop cancer,
So people do not die!

I have a dream to be me,
Because I know how
Easy and hard it can be!

Jessica Vandepeer (12)
Fulston Manor School, Sittingbourne

What's With Bullying?

What's the deal with bullying?
Why be a bully?
Why suffer the sadness of someone else?
Why deal with the fear?
Why live with the regret?
Why stick with the violence?
When will the bullying stop?
Bullies never win.

Say no to bullying!

Ryan Croall (12)
Fulston Manor School, Sittingbourne

I Have A Dream
(By the dogs at Essex's dogs' home)

Alone, alone
All on my own
Not a care in the world
Not even a look my way

Help me, love me
Care for me, feed me
Help me out, get me out

I need a carer
I need an owner
Feed me, walk me
And I will be good
Don't do this and I won't do what I should

Big dogs, small dogs
Fluffy dogs, bald dogs
Grey dogs, white dogs, black dogs

Help us, feed us, love us
Help us out, get us out.

Stephen Pink (12)
Fulston Manor School, Sittingbourne

I Have A Dream

I have a dream that all crime will stop
And will not exist.
I have a dream that I could live
Without hiding my possessions from burglars
Or avoiding the dark alleys.
I have a dream people can live freely
Without double locking things or
Spending money on extra protection.
I have a dream that one day
I will be the one to stop them!

Jack Donoghue (13)
Fulston Manor School, Sittingbourne

My Family And Me

My nan is polite,
She's kind and amusing,
She's loud but quiet,
And she's sometimes confusing.

My mum is nice,
She's helpful and smart,
And let's add another thing,
She's quite good at art.

My grandad is clever,
He used to be a cop,
Don't get on the wrong side of him,
'Cause otherwise he'll pop.

My brothers are strange,
Well, that's all I can say,
We always fight
And hardly play.

I think that I'm the weirdest of my whole family,
But I don't really care 'cause that's just me!

Bobbie Cornelius (12)
Fulston Manor School, Sittingbourne

Beautiful Earth

War is not always the answer
Try to use words rather than violence
Don't allow fear to make your feelings show
Allow fear to do what is right
Never make yourself scared and small
Make yourself bold and tall

Say what you think about what is right and wrong
Don't allow your feelings to bubble up inside you
Like a shaken bottle of fizzy drink
Allow them to pass through you
Like a gentle breeze through a forest of trees

Be the one who makes people happy
Be the one in a dark room
Showing people the way to go

When the day ends
You can finally be happy
In a happy, pleasant world

Beautiful Earth.

Stephanie Smith (13)
Fulston Manor School, Sittingbourne

Dreams

Dreams
To win CPSA world championship

Dreams
Things that can calm you down

Dreams
To become a policeman

Dreams
Happening all around

Dreams
To climb Everest

Dreams
Things that can turn you around

Dreams
To become a CPSA referee

Dreams
Can change the world.

Ricky Telford (11)
Fulston Manor School, Sittingbourne

I Dreamed

I dreamed about being famous
I dreamed about being fast
I dreamed about being the world's best
I dreamed of holding the record
I dreamed of being her.

My dream said I would be her
If I kept doing what I do
I'm nearly where she is
800m, that's not far
Off I go . . . zoom!

Lilly Coward (12)
Fulston Manor School, Sittingbourne

Racism

Racism is a bad thing when people say it to you,
You feel anger, tears, disliked, inequality and frustrated.

I wish to say the same thing back,
To the people who racially abuse me,
But I know that if I said anything, I would be as bad as them.

But we should come together and fight to stop racism
Like Michael Jackson once said,
'It don't matter if you're black or white'.

Events of the past like the slave trade and apartheid
Should be forgotten and we as a nation should move on
And teach our children to live in harmony
And discourage racial tension.

As Martin Luther King once imagined that one day
White brothers and black brothers would play together
And that his four little children would one day live in a nation
Where they would not be judged by the colour of their skin
But by the content of their character.

Tanaka Mtisi (12)
Fulston Manor School, Sittingbourne

Poverty Poem

Pain today, pain tomorrow
It lingers today
Many people pray
That the world will change.
They wish for a house with a door
With more money for the poor.
Green grass
Looks nicer than brass.
Make the punishment fit the crime
Help the Third World
And be proud.

Ryan Mallion (12)
Fulston Manor School, Sittingbourne

I Have A Dream

I have a dream that never ends,
If ever we fight, we'll make amends.
The war and peace, we'll fight for rights,
If things go wrong, we'll hold on tight.

If you want answers, don't turn to crime,
If you fight boredom, don't take what's mine,
Look to the future and learn to toe the line.

You get from life what you put in,
If you do the crime then you do the time.
You'll get one chance, so do your best,
Remember this is it, there is no test.

Live every day like it's your last,
So look to the future and not your past.
Stare out your window and what do you see?
The sky is blue, so is the sea.
Respect this world and all around,
And that's how it should be.

Evelyn Irwin (12)
Fulston Manor School, Sittingbourne

I Have A Dream

My dream is to climb a mountain
That reaches way up into the sky.
The mountains will just get higher and higher
And will never stop growing.
And when I get to the top
I can feel proud that I've made it this far
And I would be so high up
That I could reach out and touch space
And see all the stars
And never have to come down again.
But I have to because I want to climb the next one!

Eddie Lovell (12)
Fulston Manor School, Sittingbourne

Dream

I dreamed I played football,
Scoring that winning goal,
For the best team in the world,
Chelsea.

A quick pass in,
Set me up perfectly,
That final touch,
Sent the ball gliding,
Straight at the goal.

Goalkeeper dove,
But narrowly missed,
As the ball soared,
Straight past him.

Final minute glory,
Everyone cheers,
'We've done it,
We've won!'

Chris Clark (11)
Fulston Manor School, Sittingbourne

My Dream

I have a dream that I will fly a jet plane
I have a dream that I will see the Earth from under my feet
I have a dream that people will see the world differently
And see it in more greatness
I have a dream that we will look after our planet for evermore
Why are we polluting our oceans and making our sea creatures suffer?
I have a dream that this will stop
I have a dream that the world will be in peace
And the wars will end forever
I have a dream that the animals of our world can live in peace
I have a dream that we can all live in peace.

Joseph Carlow (12)
Fulston Manor School, Sittingbourne

I Have A Dream

A dream in the night has me playing the beautiful
Game of football. My name is famous all around
The world and when I score and pass all the crowd
Shout it out.

A dream in the night is me as a police officer helping
The innocent and protecting all people that may need
It. Patrolling the streets to keep them safe any time
Day or night.

A dream in the night has me in camouflage trying to put
A stop to all wars and helping the innocent people protect
Their families and homes when needed.

A dream in the night is me trying to change the world
Making it a greener place where people can live their
Lives without pollution and poverty.

A dream in the night is only a dream until I awake and
Then reality hits me because I'm only me again.

Jordan Spicer (12)
Fulston Manor School, Sittingbourne

I Have A Dream

Think deeply
No racism
Think hard
No fighting in the world,
It's a better place
Think now
The children in Africa
Having food, water and education
Think more
Stop pollution
Just think
We could make this happen.

Lauren Gridley (12)
Fulston Manor School, Sittingbourne

Dreams Are Possible

Dreams are possible,
I believe in dreams.

Every fly and bumblebee,
Everything you see,
Every human and animal,
Should live in harmony.

Hurting, anger or sadness,
Should be turned into glee and happiness,
Lonely, sad and crying
And everybody dying.

Poverty, war and fighting should be banned,
For a life in a better land.
If we all worked hard together,
We all could be friends forever.

Dreams are possible,
Do you have a dream?

Melody Butcher (13)
Fulston Manor School, Sittingbourne

I Have A Dream

I have a dream that I am a wrestling superstar,
Fight my opponent and try my best,
Like Rey Mysterio or John Cina
Who are world wrestling superstars.
I have a dream that I am a famous superbike racer
I try my best to win trophies to put in my trophy cabinet
And to be a world champion superbike racer
And for everyone to know who I am
And be able to be on telly all the time.
I have a dream to help our country and other countries
By taking lots of food and water over there
So they don't die of starvation or dehydration.

Ryan Card (11)
Fulston Manor School, Sittingbourne

I Dream Of A Happy World

I dream of a healthy and powerful world,
Would it be healthy, would it be peaceful?
Is the world still well held?
I don't know so I wrote this speech.

Will the people still have happiness
Or will they have sadness?
Will children play
Or will they live in clay?

Will the animals live?
What could we give?
Could we give care,
Or would we just scare?

What could the world become,
If we all succumb?
Would we change
The world today?

Lily Tonner (11)
Fulston Manor School, Sittingbourne

I Have A Dream

I have a dream,
I hope you're here,
Not too far or not too near,
To have you close,
I want the most,
You're in my heart forever and ever,
Maybe one day my pain will go,
Once I know you're watching over me,
My tears will drop from my face,
To know the happiness has come,
With such a great grace.

RIP, Max.

Harley Provan (12)
Fulston Manor School, Sittingbourne

St Katherine's Docks

I would quite happily live in a flat,
If I could live in St Katherine's docks,
It's an amazing place to be,
Peaceful, tranquil, so very me.

Boats toing and froing since 1827,
Vibrant coloured sailing boats, all shapes and sizes,
Magnificent luxury yachts moored along the quay,
A wonderful vision for all to see.

Historic buildings surround the docks,
Trees swaying in the breeze,
Graceful, Cillit Bang white swans,
Swimming gracefully.

Living in my penthouse suite,
Overlooking St Katherine's docks,
When I finally get there,
I'll know I've achieved a lot.

Amy Bowling (11)
Fulston Manor School, Sittingbourne

I Had A Dream

I had a dream where everything was made of ice cream,
The world lived on cheese that was a real please.
A world where cowboys pushed their luck
And everyone had a pet duck.
Boys had ponytails covered with snails,
Where girls ruled the world and everybody's hair was curled.
We all know the world isn't like this,
But if it was it would be big.
Around the world there would be fun
For everything and everyone.
That was my dream, but it never came true,
Now I am feeling very blue!

Aimee Pelling (12)
Fulston Manor School, Sittingbourne

I Have A Dream

I have a dream
I will be the best drummer ever
I have a dream
I will have the best drum set
It will be shiny with steel and chrome
I have a dream
I will hear the music
I have a dream
I will beat the drums in time
I have a dream
The music will keep going because of me
I have a dream
Because
I'm
The
Best
That's my dream.

William Reynolds (12)
Fulston Manor School, Sittingbourne

I Have A Dream

I have a dream that one day bullying will stop
That people won't be frightened
And the world will be a better place.

I have a dream that one day I will be able to do what I want,
Without having to worry what others may think.

I have a dream that everyone will be happy,
Living without fear of others, everyone will be nice.

I have a dream that one day I will be driving trains
Just like my grandad, not worrying what others think.

I have a dream that one day bullying will come to an end
And I will finally be able to become me.

Daniel Elliott (13)
Fulston Manor School, Sittingbourne

Dreams

I'm lying in bed one night
My bed covers really tight
I dream about being a football player
Like the ones on TV
I wish I played for Arsenal
Especially like the ex-players such as Thierry Henry
I would earn lots of money and buy a Ferrari
I'm lying in bed dreaming about me
Especially when I'm playing with Van Persie
And Gael Clichy would be coming to the pub with me
I would have a big mansion with all my family
I don't want my dream to end
Smiling inside and feeling very happy
And then I wake up and realise that I'm being very dappy
Whilst having breakfast
I think about my dream and all the funny things
And I know if I proceed, I will succeed.

Jake March (12)
Fulston Manor School, Sittingbourne

Family

I have a dream that my parents will get back together,

Family

I have a dream that my great nan will come back to life

Family

I have a dream that I can make my family happy

Family

I have a dream that there is a difference in my family

Why my
Family?

Lauren Bampton (12)
Fulston Manor School, Sittingbourne

My Dreams Of Wonder!

I dream when I grow,
Aim high, never low,
Grow big or tall,
Grow short or small,
Always try your best, being better than the rest,
When I grow old,
I dream of achieving my goals.

When I grow I dream of winning,
I loved horse riding from the very beginning,
I learnt from the start,
It's deep in my heart,
My dream is to compete for gold,
With my hair in a bun, having so much fun,
It's now I know my life has just begun.

I do love kids and of course I wouldn't want to miss,
The special times of being a mum.

Katie Denny (12)
Fulston Manor School, Sittingbourne

I Have A Dream

I have a dream that bullying will stop,
Mickey-taking out of kids that are different,
Groups of kids that overpower them,
I dream it will happen.

I have a dream that people will be treated fairly,
No matter their size and colour,
Child or adult,
I dream it will happen.

I have a dream fighting will cease,
The world will be at ease,
No arguing, no fighting,
I dream it will happen.

Shannara Harrild (12)
Fulston Manor School, Sittingbourne

I Have A Dream To Be Just Like My . . .

I have a dream to be just like my dad,
Kind, funny and caring,
Inspirational and brilliant,
Clever and cool.

I have a dream to be just like my mum,
Silly, weird and funny,
Strange and unusual,
Helpful, caring and kind.

I have a dream to be just like my sister,
Feisty, cool and brilliant,
Caring and kind,
Funny and amusing.

I have a dream to be just like my brother,
    Not really!

I have a dream to be just like me!

Amy Dixon (12)
Fulston Manor School, Sittingbourne

I Have A Dream

I have a dream
That the world is clean
Stop being a bully
Stop hiding in your hoodie
I have a dream
That the world is clean
That litter is gone
And we keep recycling along
I have a dream
That we stop all wars
Stop hiding on the floors
Stop holding the guns
Just have fun.

Luke Brooks (13)
Fulston Manor School, Sittingbourne

I Have A Dream

I wish I could be a designer,
For nothing could be finer
Than making my own car,
One that would take me far.
Nothing could be sweeter,
Than driving my two seater,
Driving it real fast,
Good times are meant to last.

I'll drive my car forever,
No matter what the weather,
I'll drive it down the highway,
Then I'll have it my way,
With the big engine roaring,
The journey won't be boring,
To park my car will cause me sorrow,
But I'll be driving again tomorrow.

Alex Corden (12)
Fulston Manor School, Sittingbourne

Poem

It might be easy to want to fight
But think of all those families in fright

All those families who care
All those children in a scare
Waiting for their daddy to come back home
He does not even have a telephone

Iraq to Afghanistan
What more to come?
We could be spending our money
On homes and hospitals
Not bullets and guns.

So please stop the wars.

Joe Timmons (12)
Fulston Manor School, Sittingbourne

I Want To Change The World

I love to change the world
To make it a better place
It's all about the base
All the different things
Starts with just a ping
Learn to love each other
Like he is your brother
I want everything to change
I know it might be strange
Their homes may be sunny
But people need the money
They are living on the streets
When their parents give the beats
I want to change everything
They only have one desperate thing
It's for you to help them through everything.

Jessica Lees (13)
Fulston Manor School, Sittingbourne

I Have A Dream . . .

To be a footballer, to be a star
To show everyone who I am
To play for Chelsea and be really wealthy
To keep myself healthy

These things I need to achieve
And to succeed
I have got to
Work hard training
Even when it's raining
Give up all things I love
Give up my other clubs
To concentrate on one thing
My ambition to play for Chelsea.

Brad Saunders (12)
Fulston Manor School, Sittingbourne

I Have A Dream: Family

I have a dream that one day
My dad could stop working hard,
Dreams
I have a dream that my mum
Will always be happy,
Dreams
I have a dream that my sister
Will always do well in school,
Dreams
I have a dream that my family
Will always stay happy
Dreams
I always thought about myself
When I was younger, but now I am older,
I think about my friends and family more.
Dreams!

Chloe Gillett (11)
Fulston Manor School, Sittingbourne

I Have A Dream

I have a dream
That no one should starve
I have a dream
That there are no more wars
I have a dream
I want everyone happy
No one snappy
I have a dream
That all do good
I have a dream
That no one becomes homeless
I have a dream
For all of today and every day.

Joseph Tunley (12)
Fulston Manor School, Sittingbourne

My Dreams

I have tons and tons of dreams,
They would make a lot of scenes.
I want to go somewhere sunny
But I don't have any money.
I would like to go on Safari,
Driving in my shiny red Ferrari.
I want to have a fishing boat
And wear a black coat.
I would love to swim in the clear blue sea
And play on a Nintendo Wii.
I don't want to die
And never want to cry.
I want big, manly muscles
And never want to eat Brussels.
I want to be a zookeeper
And I never want to see the Grim Reaper.

Matthew Tumber (11)
Fulston Manor School, Sittingbourne

I Believe

I believe
That I had a dream
In which bullies were never seen.
Everyone's mad but no one's bad,
I believe,
I believe

That I had a dream
Where racism had never been
And everyone stood up tall
Like a broad bean

I believe.

Dylan Lee (13)
Fulston Manor School, Sittingbourne

I Have A Dream

I dream about change,
Change that no more soldiers
Will hit the ground cold and motionless.
I dream that there will be no more racism in the world.
We are all the same people inside.
We may not have the same colour skin,
Why does it matter what colour your skin is?

When I grow up I dream that I'm going to be an artist.
How they paint with expression,
How every last detail is perfect.
When their steady hand hits the page, it turns magical.
How every painting turns out great.

There are good and bad lives.
Bad lives are like unfinished paintings.
I just hope they'll be finished soon.

Millie Nash (11)
Fulston Manor School, Sittingbourne

When I Grow Up

I have a dream of being a pop star
One day I hope I will go far.

Make lots of money and travel the world
Wear lots of make-up and have my hair curled.

Being in a girl band is my ideal dream
Where I hope I will be seen.

Wear big diamonds and bright coloured clothes
Wear high-heeled shoes with painted toes.

The Saturdays and Atomic Kitten . . .
Being a pop star - I'm really smitten!

Kyah Dooley (12)
Fulston Manor School, Sittingbourne

Power To Change

I look at the world
And what do I see?
A world full of violence and poverty.
I am a teenage girl,
But I have the power to change the world.

With a planet full of violence,
Drugs and war,
I wonder when they'll learn,
But all they seem to care about
Is how much they will earn.

I watch the news and I start to muse,
Why do they do nothing?
Don't they understand?
If we work together,
We can live in a brighter land!

Beth Tumber (13)
Fulston Manor School, Sittingbourne

My Dream

My dream is to see a world
Free from cigarettes and drugs.
All they do is wreck your life
And they can kill.
The answer to drugs and cigarettes
Is no!

They're killing our country,
They're killing our people,
They're killing our continents,
They're killing the world.

Ellis Bell (13)
Fulston Manor School, Sittingbourne

In The World

In the world there is
Death and pain and sadness.

There is torture,
Violence and grief,
Starvation and misery.

In the world there is
The blue sky, the rainbows
And happiness.

If I could change the world I would not,
For if the world was perfect,
Why would we need hope and faith?

I shall have hope and faith,
For that is what will make the world
Turn into tomorrow.

Hannah Haith (12)
Fulston Manor School, Sittingbourne

I Had A Dream

I had a dream
In which the world was all clean
Where rivers were clear and fields were green
The air was sweet
And safe for children to meet
No bullets, no bombs
No hate, no wars
I had a dream.

I had a dream
That the world was all dirty
Where rivers were murky and fields were concrete
The air was grey, no place to play
Bullets, bombs, hate, war
This is not a dream
It's reality!

Holly Smith (12)
Fulston Manor School, Sittingbourne

I Have A Dream

I have a dream where birds can sing
And one day I could fly with them
I have a dream to act the scene
I have a dream to fly away
And be at peace with everything.

I have a dream where the world is free
And where we no longer cut down trees
I have a dream of a clear sky
And of a world where no one dies.

I have a dream that you now understand
So listen to my words
And be at peace with the land.

I have a dream that will never die
As long as that lives, so will I.

Jordan Maddison (12)
Fulston Manor School, Sittingbourne

Dream And Ambition

When I grow up and am a man,
My dream would be to fly over the land.
To be a pilot and fly a jet,
I would soar through the sky above the clouds.
My dream would make me proud.
I would also like to end world violence,
But I know that might never happen.

But if this does not happen,
I would like to play for Manchester United
And play at Old Trafford,
The place they call 'The Theatre of Dreams'
And my skills would be as good as Ronaldo
And I'd score the goals and get us up the table.
Then I would quit that and become a manager.

Chey Caulfield (11)
Fulston Manor School, Sittingbourne

Fantasy

I had a dream
Of country cottages
And clotted cream,
A field of corn, a field of wheat,
The sight of lambs with a gentle bleat.

A farmhouse smell with fresh baked bread,
A bale of hay to rest my head,
The dew that's lying on the ground,
The mature manure in a great big mound.

The clanging of a bell hanging from a cow,
Getting nearer, what a row!
Just not stopping, won't go away.

It's my alarm for another . . .
School day!

Alice McLaughlin (12)
Fulston Manor School, Sittingbourne

I Have A Dream

I have a dream that racism is not in the world,
Because I think it's cruel and mean.

When I grow up I would love to be an actress
Because I love performing on stage.
I would not like animals to be locked up in a cage.

I would like everyone to have a home
And not live on the streets.

I would love to meet Simon Webbe
Because I think he's a great singer.

I would not like anyone to starve or be thirsty
Because they could die and not survive,
Even if they were bad people.

I dream that all of this will happen.

Kerri White (12)
Fulston Manor School, Sittingbourne

I Have A Dream

Young, talented and pretty - so lucky, lucky, lucky
Australian with attitude - and we wouldn't change a thing
Struck down with cancer - strong, determined and plucky
Put yourself in her place - spinning around - scared, frightened
So unlucky!
Can't get it out of her head - but family saying confide in us
Tears on her pillow but the battle was won
She did it again and rose from the ashes
To make more hits, especially for you
Taking things slow - 'give me just a little more time'
To become the red-blooded woman we all love and know
Her world is enriched - perfumes and chocolate
With her adoring fans saying, 'I believe in you'
A showgirl tour and a duet with Robbie
And we all came into her world for a celebration of life.

Faye Davis-Smith (12)
Fulston Manor School, Sittingbourne

Imagine

Imagine
Meeting Dani Harmer, the actress.
Imagine
Riding a dolphin across the Atlantic Ocean.
Imagine
The first time looking at your brand new horse.
Imagine
Helping horses all day long
Imagine
Going on your very first holiday.
Imagine
Being a vet and treating all the sick animals.
Imagine
Stopping global warming.
Imagine.

Maizy Brackley (12)
Fulston Manor School, Sittingbourne

War

Imagine no soldiers, imagine no homes
Imagine children living alone.
Imagine no racism, imagine no wars
Would there ever be a place without war?

Imagine a world with no knives, no guns
A place where no one must hide, or even run
Imagine being as free as a bird
Even being in a crowd of soldiers
Your voice will still be heard.

The days of death
The haunting nights
The night he lives
The day he dies
Soon he begs for mercy
In front of the Devil's eyes.

Sharmin Gafoor (12)
Harris Academy, Merton

Racism

Racism
People are getting bullied
Racism
People are getting shot
Racism
People are attacked because of their colour
Imagine
A world without racism
Imagine
When the world is one
Imagine
A world of freedom
Inspire
A world without hatred
Inspire
A world with no fear
Inspire
A world with no grief
Imagine
A world like this.

Emma-Louise Hawkins (13)
Harris Academy, Merton

Racism

What about my colour?
Why does it matter to you?
Is it 'cause I'm black, white or Asian?
Just because I'm different, just because I'm new.

We all came from the same pot,
We are all babies in the same cot.
We are all tied together in the same knot,
You think we are different but we're not.

We are all linked by the same chain,
Doesn't matter that we have a different name.
In our hearts we are all the same,
Feeling each other's happiness, feeling each other's pain.

What about my colour?
Why does it matter to you?
Is it 'cause I'm black, white or Asian?
Just because I'm different, just because I'm new.

CJ Carrington, Sara Goddard (12), Amber, Paige, Kevin & Florence
Harris Academy, Merton

War

War makes people homeless and poor,
War is like Hell knocking at your door.
When you have nowhere to run,
Your only choice is to fight.

Against many opponents the sky turns grey,
It feels like today is Judgement Day.
The end is nigh.

Clash, boom, pow! That is the sound of a gun,
One shot of that and you will surely be gone.
Soldiers think that they can win,
But all hope goes straight in the bin.
The end is nigh.
War has to stop right now,
To stop that clash, *boom, pow!*

Bryant Wachsmann, Joshua Yansen, O'Shane Braham & Charlie Seymour
Harris Academy, Merton

Racism

Racism
People are getting bullied
Racism
People are getting shot
Racism
Kids are attacked because of their race
Imagine
A world without racism
Imagine
A world where everyone is one
Imagine
A world of freedom
Inspire
A world with no hatred
Inspire
A world with no fear
Inspire
A world with no grief
Imagine
A world like that.

Charlie Ensor
Harris Academy, Merton

Today

Today I have a dream
A dream that I'll become a leader of a team.
A dream that I'll become a speaker with a crowd.
A dream that I'll be free to have fun and shout out loud.

A dream when I'll be able to live a day without a beating.
A dream when I receive a kindly greeting.
A day when I'm allowed to smile and laugh.
A dream when I'll be able to learn science and read a graph.

A dream when I'm allowed to love.
A dream when I don't get pushed or shoved.
A dream when someone notices me.
A dream when I never beg or plea.

A dream when one day I enjoy my life.
A dream when I'm not just a beaten wife.
A dream when people take me into consideration.
A dream when I forget my fury and frustration.

A dream that there will be more survivors out there.
A dream that they find people who care.
A dream when families don't kill their wives and daughters.
A dream that everything is as clear as the waters.

A dream when girls being born is not a disgrace.
A dream when you can choose who to love and embrace.
A dream when you don't have to walk with your eyes to the floor.
A dream to find people that listen and open their door.

A dream when your father is proud to call you his child.
A dream when a family, a home are beguiled.
A dream when you are worth more than cows.
A dream when a husband keeps his vows.

I have a dream that someday women will be treated as equal
                                                    as men,
I have a dream that beating women will not be as common as
                                                    one in ten.

Saveena Mangat (14)
Heathland School, Hounslow

Persephone's Dream

I sit below the pomegranate tree,
Watching the souls drift past,
I see children murdered for their race,
Women dead of starvation or sickness,
Men butchered by bloody wars,
One little creature scarcely looks human.
Wide eyes staring from a skeletal face,
Stomach bloated with hunger,
Still wailing for one last morsel,
And I wonder where is worse?
This dark underworld, watching grey ghosts,
Or the world above where chaos reigns,
Just six more pomegranate seeds
Would have freed me from that world . . .
A sudden quiet breaks my reverie.
The baby's mother has soothed it to sleep.
She smiles at me,
A strange sight on a skull-like face.
How can she smile after such suffering?
'I have hope,' she replies.
'For the sons of my sisters, my brothers' daughters,
Hope that they can end the suffering in my land.'
If the dead can hope,
There is still hope for the living,
And for me.

Charlotte Smith (14)
Heathland School, Hounslow

I Have A Dream

I had a dream
He had one too
That could change the lives
Of him, her, me, them and you
A dream that would hopefully someday come true
Mine was like his and I want it to pursue

I have a dream to stop all this war
He did too and believed once before
He stopped the tears, the screaming and blood
He stopped the guns and people dying in the mud
Mahatma Gandhi was his name
He did something good, not trying to achieve fame
He just wanted this all to cease
So he could fill the world with joy, love and peace

If you have a dream, don't give up
Keep trying and trying, don't depend on luck
And one day your dream, like mine, will come true
It could change the lives of him, her, me, them and you.

Dhanya Acharya (14)
Heathland School, Hounslow

I Have A Dream

One day maybe they will see,
Us for who we are not who we used to be,
They look at us with stereotypical minds,
Oh, how I wish they could shut those biased blinds.

A new day on the horizon,
Will any of them commit treason?
They think they are a higher class,
Oh, won't this prejudice ever pass?

We're just as good as they are,
Their state of mind is bizarre,
We should all be treated equally,
But every day opens the page to this enduring sequel.

I have a dream and maybe one day it will come true,
This is the dream I am destined to pursue,
I wish to see a happier day for us all,
A day when we connect like an urban sprawl.

Karisma Pankhania (14)
Heathland School, Hounslow

I Have A Dream

In my dreams I am a game creator,
I have created a game about Zelda.

In my dreams I am thinking of my game.

In my dreams I am rich to buy all the games.

In my dreams I create my Yu-gi-oh!
It is a powerful card.

In my dreams, I'm a runner,
I run round the track.

Daniel Compton-Williams (14)
Holyport Manor School, Holyport

I Have A Dream . . .

I will fly to Africa
I will see the sun
I will see all the animals
There is sand
Everything is dry
I hear birds
I hear crickets
I smell blossoms
I also smell
Things that rot
There is a baby elephant
He's lost
Where is his mum?
Someone has taken her tusks
She's gone!
I go to the baby
'I will look after you'
I stroke her
'I will help you
Keep calm'
It starts to rain
The wind is blowing
The baby is scared
She follows me.

Natalie Helm (15)
Holyport Manor School, Holyport

In My Dreams

In my dreams I am in a jet,
Soaring high above the clouds, no need to fret.
I am heading to California, the state of dreams,
It is so hot there, I might just eat some ice creams.
Diving through the clear blue seas, hopefully won't freeze.
Standing there, feeling the warm summer breeze.
Me and Arnold Schwarzenegger having a talk,
While we're walking down the Hollywood star walk.
Sitting on the beach eating pear,
Feeling the cool summertime air.
In Las Vegas staying at the MGM Grand,
The finest hotel in all the land.
In a helicopter, going sky high,
Must eat an American apple pie.
Me in the sun, sipping some wines,
Enjoying the sight of the lovely vines.
On my way home now after all that fun,
Hopefully, one day I will return to the state of the sun.

Martin Doyle (14)
Holyport Manor School, Holyport

I Have A Dream

In my dreams
I am on holiday in Morocco

In my dreams
I am on a sandy beach

In my dreams
I am having a fun time

In my dreams
I see lots of sunshine.

Adam Hassani (14)
Holyport Manor School, Holyport

I Have A Dream

In my dreams I am a hairdresser
I win a big competition to be the hairdresser of the year.

In my dreams I am an air hostess
I am serving champagne.

In my dreams I am a policewoman
I have just arrested a burglar.

In my dreams I am a dancer
I am on stage with the Pussycat Dolls and the audience love me.

In my dreams I am a vet
I save a horse's life.

In my dreams I am in the equestrian Olympic team
I have won a gold medal.

In my dreams I'm so many people,
I wonder what I really would be . . .?

Lauren Way (13)
Holyport Manor School, Holyport

I Have A Dream

I would love to live in a mansion
And play computer games on my widescreen TV
My mansion is the biggest in England
It has ten king size bedrooms
With a candy machine in each one
All my friends stay over whenever they like
We have pillow fights and watch scary films
In the summer we'll cook a barbeque
I'll have my own art studio
Where I'll paint my masterpieces
Burglars beware!
My security guards have big muscles
And my guard dogs are quick!

David Harber (15)
Holyport Manor School, Holyport

In My Dreams Poem

In my dreams I am on an adventure
Searching in different areas.

In my dreams I am seeing a vampire who is always up to no good
Killing and drinking blood from other human beings.

In my dreams I see myself slipping away from my own grasp
Which makes me feel devastated.

In my dreams I feel angry inside
I sometimes want to let it all go.

In my dreams I feel angry inside
Sometimes bad things happen.

In my dreams I've been practising cricket
Improving my batting and bowling.

In my dreams I see myself scoring a turkey
In ten-pin bowling - this is three strikes in a row.

Matthew Pearson (15)
Holyport Manor School, Holyport

A House Full Of Animals

I have a dream, a house full of animals,
To care for them and to visit the vets.
My animals, they fill each room,
A bigger house I'll need quite soon.

Each of them has a separate view,
To bring calm and peace to me and you.
They may be animals, hamsters and cats,
But they each have character, of course I know that.

So I'll play with them daily,
Look after their needs,
And if they have accidents,
I'll mop up their pees!

James McGreevy (15)
Holyport Manor School, Holyport

My Dream

My dream
I have a dream!
I would like a car.
The car is black, it is huge,
It is a convertible, it has a badge,
It is a Volvo.
I like my car, it looks good,
I like to drive fast,
The roof is down,
The wind runs through my hair,
The radio is on very loud.
The sky is blue, not any clouds,
There are lots of people all around,
I drive my car,
It makes lots of sound,
I hope this dream comes true!

Usmaan Khan (15)
Holyport Manor School, Holyport

I Have A Dream

In my dreams I am a rugby star.

In my dreams I am a copper
I am catching a burglar.

In my dreams I am a fighter
A kick boxing champion.

In my dreams I am in a football team
I'm going to the World Cup.

In my dreams I am rich and famous
I drive a rocket car.

In my dreams I am a bartender.

In my dreams I have a Lamborghini Gallardo
I drive it really fast on the motorway.

I do lots of things in my dreams.

Arron Lewis (13)
Holyport Manor School, Holyport

In My Dreams

In my dream,
I see Sonicformers.

In my dream,
I see planet Cyber-movius.

In my dream,
I see Autosonic and Deceptisonic.

In my dream,
I see Optimus Prime and Megatron.

In my dream,
They fight each other.

In my dream,
I wake up excited.

Esther Currey (13)
Holyport Manor School, Holyport

I Have A Dream

My boyfriend
His hair and how good looking
He is!
We went to London
His dad said, 'Yes you can
Don't be late!'
We saw the lights
We saw bikes and Big Ben
We went to the London Eye
I was frightened
He said,
'You will be alright
Just come on in it
Just cuddle me and you'll be safe!'

Katy Mills (15)
Holyport Manor School, Holyport

This Is My Dream

I have a dream
That children will be equal
Not to die when they are foetal
That children will be people

I have a dream
That people will be kind
So happiness and love are theirs to find

I have a dream
That kids will have an education
Not run like automation

I have a dream
That people will have zeal
And also have a good meal

This is my dream.

Stephan Liennard (13)
Meadows School, Tunbridge Wells

Luke's Dream

I have a dream
That I will be a successful skier.

I have a dream
That I will be the next best BMX rider.

I have a dream
That one day everyone can get on with each other.

I have a dream
That there will be no school.

I have a dream
That it will stop raining in England.

I have a dream
That some day the world will be a better place.

Luke Williams (13)
Moor House School, Oxted

My Dream

My dream is wonderful
Because it is a good dream
In my dream
People are flying in the sky
Looking down
At houses, cars, bikes, shops and people walking.

In my dream
Are lots of animals
Like dogs, cats and horses
All the animals in the world
Are helping me
The animals are sleeping
Next to me and next to the trees.

In my dream
Is a hero
Called Superman
Who saves the day
He is helping me
He sees a girl
Walking on the path
A car is going to crash into her
And Superman is flying to the rescue.

I like my dreams
Because I can be going to the shops
Or having a posh limousine
In front of the house
In my dream
I want to be famous.

Elizabeth McKinnon-Green (14)
Moor House School, Oxted

I Have A Dream!

I will be famous and notable
I will make lots of money
And be able to change the world

I will care for myself
And others who are lonely
And need support

If I have children
My children will have a home
Food, a good environment
And a better life
My children will have a big future

We are living in a world
Where we don't look after the environment
And have horrible violence
We must treat ourselves
As good human beings
Stop the violence
And change our community

My hero
Is Barack Obama
The first black American president in history
I hope he'll make
Our lives healthier and strong
For the world.

Paul Davordzie-Banini (14)
Moor House School, Oxted

Future Dream

F ighting and killing
U nhappy people living on the streets suffering
T housands of soldiers dead each and every day
U nhappy wives telling their husbands to not go, but stay
R avaged countries seeking power
E ven to me all of this is sour

   No! That's not the dream I want, this is:

D amaged houses, countries fighting no more and nowhere
R emember, no more of the horror, make sure that no one needs to care
E veryone is free
A dream I want is a nice world with fields, plants and trees, people playing and full of bees
M ight and power can be strong things, but not as strong as love and peace. Hate and war, they just destroy the world, so let's help each other out and bring an end.

Shaid Coventon Webb (13)
Moor House School, Oxted

What An Unfair World!

I had a dream
That the whole world would change
I had a dream
That people won't need to suffer
I had a dream
That people won't be greedy and others can be fed
I had a dream
That people led equal lives and had equal rights
I had a dream
God would teach us all how to live
But it's just a dream
They don't always happen.

Kane Burns (14)
Moor House School, Oxted

I Have A Dream

I dream of being a great chef
I practise cooking
Cutting and peeling
Trying not to burn the food

I'd like to cook for famous people
And have my own restaurant
With more chefs
Waiters and waitresses

When I am a great chef
I would have lots of money
And be rich
It would be nice to have some children
And I hope they are nice to me!
What they do with their lives is up to them
And their dreams.

Katrina Payne (13)
Moor House School, Oxted

I Have A Dream

I have a dream
I want to play for a team
Called Chelsea FC
As a goalkeeper
Go in the pool every day
After the training session
All day Saturday
Playing matches
Half-time in the changing room
Listening to the shouts
Going to the pub after the match
Back to training session
Having physio.

Caoimhe Patterson (14)
Moor House School, Oxted

Creative Future

Creativity,
Is a whole selection of things,
From graphics to sculpting,
Painting to designing,
But I always dreamed of becoming an artist,
And creating my very own graphic novels,
Even though it is a tricky job to do,
So I will still carry on,
To succeed at my goal
And work for a bright future.

Romany Wixon Gibbs (14)
Moor House School, Oxted

My 'I Had A Dream' Poem

On a warm, balmy night
I had a dream which was cool
It was too cool for school

It was about Jimmy, the USMC cat
He was a spy who killed flies
With a machete and pistol

He didn't care how he killed
He couldn't be bothered to use a shield
Killing for years, he began to get sad
Because poor Jimmy, the USMC cat
Had no owner's mat

But he got back on his feet
And back on his track
To kill those flies for justice in his job
For this was Jimmy, the
USMC cat!

Thomas Osland (12)
Oxted School, Oxted

Listen Here

Now listen here, Mister,
I have a dream!
To be a star on a stage,
Do you know what I mean?

The crowds would go crazy,
They'd be screaming all night long,
I'd be up there waving,
They'd know all the words to my song!

I don't care about money
And I don't care about cars,
I want them to think I'm funny -
Don't want gold bars!

Please Sir,
Just let me try to explain,
I'm not looking for girls
Or all the fortune and fame . . .

I want a career
I'd enjoy every day,
So let me be a musician -
Don't get in my way!

Jacob Allen (14)
Oxted School, Oxted

Make It Stop

Child abuse,
Make it stop.
If you know someone being abused,
Make it stop.
Be a good friend,
Make it stop.
Tell an adult so they can,
Make it stop.

Matt Phillips (12)
Oxted School, Oxted

If Your Dream . . .

If your dream made the world go round
Making change without a sound
If your dream grew the trees and flowers
If your dream had such great powers
If your dream made the whole world sing
If your dream gave the birds their wing
If your dream made the north wind blow
If your dream gave the sun its glow
If your dream gave love at first sight
And for that love it gave the night
If your dream brought a sunny day
If your dream made the tall trees sway
If your dream gave a gasp for joy
If your dream made each girl and boy
If your dream brought people whom we love
If your dream brought the snow-white dove
And all the living things that roam
And giving them a happy home
So when it's time to go to bed
Create those things within your head.

Brogan Smith (12)
Oxted School, Oxted

Happiness

Happiness is fickle,
It is always ending,
But if it was any longer,
Would we enjoy it so?
Even with the plagues and horrors on the planet,
Without them, happiness we might not know.

William Eves (14)
Oxted School, Oxted

Untitled

War is a thing that goes on in life.
You go in alive but come out in a body bag.
War has been around for centuries.
We lose and win so many times.

War is a commitment,
Swearing your life for your country
And only fighting to win and not to lose.
When war happens, men run,
Grab their guns and fight
And never give up.

War is war and war will never stop.

William Gottelier (13)
Oxted School, Oxted

Imagine

Stopping criminals takes up my time,
Thieves, robbers, preventing crime.

Flying around 24/7,
It's simply great, like living in Heaven.

The look on their faces when they see me there,
As if I were a grizzly bear.

I'll continue this job as long as I can,
Since I'm no average guy, I am the Batman.

Imagine . . .

Dominic Nolan (14)
Oxted School, Oxted

My Desire

My desire is for this war to come to an end,
For this bloodshedding to stop,
It can't commence,
It is too much for the children to see.

My desire is for these nations to come together,
For them to help each other in difficult times,
And not fight for what is not rightfully theirs,
For them to share the land equally, for it is the Earth's nature.

My desire is for everyone to join hands together,
For us to see each other in the same category,
For us to walk the land freely as a bird,
And not fear for our lives to be taken away.

My desire is for different races of people
To smile at each other and drink lemonade in the sun,
For the eyes of the racist to be cleaned,
For them to have a clear view of everyone.

My desire is for the animals to live in peace,
For them not to fear the poacher carrying away their heritage,
For them to roam freely in the land that is theirs and ours,
For them to drink from the pond without looking twice because of the pollution.

My desire is for my grandchildren to play in their backyard,
For them to ride their bikes in the streets laughing,
For me not to worry that they might get a certain disease,
My desire is strong and passionate.

Khadija Kassim (12)
Prendergast Ladywell Fields College, London

Untitled

The world needs help
I hear its dreams
Covered and muffled in silence and screams
Help the world
Let us fight
Break the routine
And put it right
I hear its dreams, so many it seems
I can't commit
My heart is open
I want to hear
But my ears are broken
I can't stand the noise
The vast loud silence
Lost magic in the art of violence
Suffered so much pain
Driven on and made to cope
Given twisted fragments of forgotten hope
I'm so broken inside
The world has nothing to offer
But much to hide
Racism, poverty is all I see
Violence, sex and guns on TV
Sometimes I wish it would stop
We could all freeze and turn back the clock
Back to simple ways
Simple days
We're so restricted
Yet so free
The world has a dream
The same with me
My dream is an enigma
Which no one can truly understand
Because it's mine
In my head
No amount of words will get it said
This needs action
This may need magic

My magic infused with yours
My dream past law and laws
So help me, take my hand
Let love and peace guide the land.

Shanara Bray (13)
Prendergast Ladywell Fields College, London

I Wish For

I wish for a world to end all bloodshed and crime,
Where we can use the power of voice,
We can help with the sound from our lips
And not the pain from our fists;
Knives and guns are the coward's way out.

Looking across the streets,
Where the blood is paved everywhere -
Leaving the atmosphere in pain and sorrow.
Violence is not the answer to our problems,
All it brings is more anger and distress to others.
But why must we kill lives to save lives?
Words have pushed us forward in life,
Whilst weapons just drag us back.

The deaths of innocents are a shared agony.
This torment is too much to bear,
Especially for the younger victims.
It should stop!
Innocent people are grasped by the reaper of death -
Our voice, no matter how small,
Can make a world of change.

I wish for a world where the smallest seed
Can overcome the largest tree,
Where one person can make a big difference.
I wish for a world where my dreams can come true.
I wish for a world.

Adrian Kamulegeya (11)
Prendergast Ladywell Fields College, London

Lost

They told me how to fight,
And beat people up,
They said it would be alright,
If I did what they asked.

One day I killed at least thirty people,
But if it wasn't done,
That night, my tiny little body, would have been gone . . .
I hoped and tried every day to escape, and run away from there,
But who, really, did care?

Nobody really looked at me,
A little, young girl, needed there to be.
Course I didn't like it,
But what was I to do?
There was no other place where I grew.

My parents were killed when I was just four,
Nobody could care for me, because I was so poor.
I now don't even know what family stands for,
I do know that I miss them every day, more and more.

I asked them about it,
They said, 'It's just none of your business.'
What can a child answer at that time?
'You can tell me, it's not a crime!'
One of them stood up and waved his hand in the air.
It went past my black hair.

It was enough, I had to leave,
Away from there,
I just didn't care.
Didn't care what they did,
About what I did commit.

It was a dark night, with the moon above my head,
I arrived somewhere, when the sun had set.
Happily I ended far away,
I was so proud, so proud on that day.

Now I tell my stories to everyone,
That they need to watch out, before they are gone.
I also tell my story, now, here to you,
I hope you just learned how pleased you need to be,
And how much you learned, about me . . .

Wahida Jabarzai (13)
Prendergast Ladywell Fields College, London

I Have A Dream

I had a dream
I could fly
I was so fast
So powerful

In this dream
When I was flying
All over the world

I could see everything
I could see tears
I could see racism
I could see blood
I could see crime
I could see war

But through all this evil cloud
I could still see peace

And with all the power I had
With the fragments of peace that there were
I could change

All the tears
All the racism
All the blood
All the war
Into a complete peace.

Camilla Yahaya (12)
Prendergast Ladywell Fields College, London

I Dream Of A Better Place

I dream of a place where I can be understood,
Such a place where finally
I can be myself.
Where we don't have to worry
And where we don't have to wait,
For a brighter tomorrow
And a happier today.

I dream of a place where I can paint the world
And sing to it my songs,
Where I can dance when I'm filled with joy
And where I cry
And no longer hold back my soul.

I dream of a place where we can walk down life's road
In one direction,
Walking hand in hand
And side to side,
For this world is all we need to have if we could just
Forget,
Forgive,
And believe.

Vwarhe Sodje (13)
Prendergast Ladywell Fields College, London

My Dreams

I have so many dreams:
One, no poverty
Two, no racism
Three, no bullying
Four, no gun and knife crime
Five, no jealousy
Six, no peer pressure
Seven, no betrayal
Eight, no teenage pregnancies
But the one I desire the most is
A world with no gun and knife crime
A world where I don't have to look over my back
A world where I can say I can live to see eighteen
A world where you can earn respect with no gun or knife
A world where I won't stray off my dream . . .
My dream of becoming an engineer
So what do you say?
Today, let us make a stand against gun and knife crime!

Adeyemi Osundina (13)
Prendergast Ladywell Fields College, London

My Life

They took my father
Raped my loving mother
I could see the bullet in my baby brother
The knife sticking out of my sister
The blood pouring from my brother
The tears pouring from my neighbours
The tears of sorrow
The spit in my mouth I could not swallow

I wish I lived in a world with no poverty
I want to live in a perfect world for eternity
I wish I lived in a world with no bullying, drugs, racism or diseases
Every day I pray to God, begging on my knees
Begging for a better life
Not to be hypnotised with gangs, drugs and knives
I wish they were all gone, the ones that did this
They should be begging for forgiveness.

Ahmed Salum (13)
Prendergast Ladywell Fields College, London

Shanty Town

As I walked through Shanty Town,
The sights I saw, the everlasting sound.
As I walked in the market place,
Scrutinising its living disgrace.

As I passed a rotting skull, I slipped and fell
In a rat-infested hole.
When I shed a tear for some beggars,
They chased me round thinking I was a robber.

As I witness a roof shatter
I ask myself what is the matter?

As I finished off my journey,
I realised the pain of a town called Shanty.

Lizzy Dayo (13)
Prendergast Ladywell Fields College, London

I Have A Dream

I have a dream,
That everyone can get along,
No matter their skin tone or height.
If I had a wish,
That would be it.

I have a dream,
That there are no diseases
That can kill you.
If I had a wish,
That would be it, to save the people I love.

I have a dream,
That racism won't get worse,
They will soon get along.
If I had a wish,
That would be it.

Tisharn Gordon-Josephs (12)
Prendergast Ladywell Fields College, London

A Dream To Change The World

I had a dream, I thought
No one would know
It was real.
It was a dream that no one could believe
It was a dream about me saving the world
Like Superman.

In my dream
I changed the world
By providing food for hungry people
In different countries
I saved the world by mending the ozone layer
In my dream I saved people that were dying.

I wish I could be Superman.

Aderinsola Adebanwo (12)
Prendergast Ladywell Fields College, London

I Have A Dream

Our time is one of war,
It is full of blood, of gore.
So this time, I have a dream,
In which a brilliant light will beam,
Over the darkness and fright,
A cradle of love throughout the night.
So, listen to my word,
It is as clear as a bird.
The enhancement of the humankind,
It is not too hard to keep the bind,
The humankind will be hard to dispatch
As it will have a harder back
And bigger lungs to go with that.
It will make us stronger -
Fact!

Pablo Bilton-Simon (12)
Prendergast Ladywell Fields College, London

Bee Dreams

My dream is like a fantasy
For the bees to survive
And the vorroa to die
To make honey for me
The bees must thrive
In their blue hive
Making golden honey
To pour out of the hive
It will 'bee'
The bees' knees
At this time of the year
The spring will come
And we will have fun
I have a bee dream.

Daniel Emptage (12)
Prendergast Ladywell Fields College, London

Fly Up Like A Bird

From a bad level to a good level
From rags to riches
From dirt to being cleansed
As I fly up like a bird

From war to peace
From noise to silence
From loneliness to happiness
From racism to friendship
Up as the world grows

From local to international
From nothing to something
From one to another
Up like a bird I flew
As a child I grew . . .

Rofiat Onanusi (13)
Prendergast Ladywell Fields College, London

What Would I Rather Have?

You could get two golden doves
But I would rather have a heart full of love.
You could get a diamond ring for a million pounds
And nothing less
But I would rather have a handful of happiness.
You could have all the jewellery in the world
But I would rather had my whole family together.
So as you see
If you look deep in your heart
You will find every bit of love
That's for a start
If you try your best
You will find a life full of happiness.

Andrea Teneda (13)
Prendergast Ladywell Fields College, London

My Vision

I have a whole new vision,
That people will live happily together,
The environment will be green,
The gangs will settle their differences
And find things they enjoy doing,
That there will be no more diseases,
There will be no more wars,
Eco-friendly cars and houses
And no more poverty,
This is my vision,
My will,
I will try and make
This vision become true.

Shaun Wilson (12)
Prendergast Ladywell Fields College, London

I Have A Dream

I don't want to be a millionaire
I don't want to be a lawyer
I don't want to be a footballer
I don't want to be a vicar
I don't want to be a diver
I don't want to be a poacher
I don't want to be an astronaut
I don't want to be a barrister
I don't want to be a pilot
I don't want to be a captain of a ship
I want to be a doctor
I want my life
I want to save lives.

Robbie Lock (11)
Prendergast Ladywell Fields College, London

My Poem About World Desire

I wish for the world to be a better place,
To put sense in the human race.
I wish for the world to have no wars,
To stop people starting it for no cause.

I wish for the world to be a better place,
Some people can act like a waste of space.
I wish for the world to have no starvation,
And for people to live in civilisation.

I wish for the world, for children not to live in poverty,
I wish all children had parents, to show loyalty.
I wish for the world not to be in dismay,
In the world there is hope, every day.

Moses Dike (13)
Prendergast Ladywell Fields College, London

I Dream

I dream that the world sometimes can be
A dangerous place
Guns, knives, including crime, destruction
Loved ones gone
Family, friends down in the ground
And they are not coming back.

But everything is going to change
When I'm at the scene
The world is going to change big time
I'm going to stop all of this!
Sometimes I dream I have super powers
The power to change the world!

Mehmet Mustafa (11)
Prendergast Ladywell Fields College, London

My Dream For The World

I have a dream that people will
Respect one another
I have a dream that there are no guns
And vandalism in this world
I have a dream that everyone
Is treated the same way
I have a dream that everybody
Looks up to older people
I have a dream that I can change the world
In a good way
I have a dream, one real dream
That I will be a doctor when I get older.

Lovell McCaulay (11)
Prendergast Ladywell Fields College, London

I Have A Dream

In the future I have a dream that I will play for magical Manchester United. Also to be as good as Cristiano Ronaldo.

My dream is as strong as an iceberg.
To score lots of goals.
To play as a striker for Manchester United.
To become the best on the team.

I'm holding onto my dream with all my strength.
I knock everything out of the way like a bulldozer.
I will never let my dream go.
This dream is as bright as gold.

Joshua Fricker (12)
Rush Croft Sports College, London

I Have A Dream

I have a dream,
That we can walk together in peace,
That one day we can go out at night
And not be afraid of guns and knives.

I aspire to a world
In which we can joyfully live happily ever after,
Where illness would never last
And like the dinosaurs, illness would be a thing of the past.

I wish
That poverty would finish,
That living without money and in misery
Would be in the books of history.

I believe
That one day all my dreams will be achieved,
Love, happiness, unity and good health
Would be the ways to save ourselves.

Prince K C Numa (12)
Rush Croft Sports College, London

My Dream

In the future I dream of a safe community
Where families live joyfully
And the bond between neighbours is hopefully
Not of their race but of friendship

The fruits of my dream will be fresh like a
Beautiful flower blossoming in a hopeful new world
I wait, hoping that someday my dream
Will be like a forest set ablaze
Touching the hearts of the old and young

But as I slowly awaken from my deep
Slumber, the world around me
Is like an impenetrable boulder
Rolling and flattening
My hopes and reams for now but one day
Even that boulder can't stand in my way

One day my dream will come true

I toil, tumble and turn
For my anger is like the steam whooshing
Out of a kettle as it boils the water.

I hope one day the world will be
A safer and happier place
But that day may not be today.

Zara Nadeem
Rush Croft Sports College, London

Line Of Crime

My dream is like a blossoming flower,
Sharing its beauty with the world.
Trust, safety, that is what we need.
To all people this is the sentence they plead.

E4, *bang, bang!*
That's what they say nowadays.
All you hear on the news.
Bang, bang, bang all day.

The news we hear, the things we see
Make us scared to step out the door.
We are like tunnels of endless darkness,
Always expecting more.

My dream is the brightest star in the sky,
Guiding people back to harmony,
Shedding the light.

E4, *bang, bang!*
That is not the way.
Let us all change the world today!

D'Anne Fearon (12)
Rush Croft Sports College, London

The World Is Coming To An End

The world is coming to an end
We are sending the world on a crash collision course to destruction.
Factories let off gases.
Polar ice caps melting.
The world is coming to an end; how do we defend?
Factories let off gases, killing us in masses.

Luke Williamson (14)
Rush Croft Sports College, London

I Have A Dream Poem

I want to do very well at school
Achieve my best results and reach my wonderful goal
Be with my lovely family every day
Sitting on the sofa watching TV

Succeed in secondary school and do my very best
Definitely do my exam, get a big A on the test
Go out shopping, go to McDonald's
Revise and revise. Look, cover, check.

Going to school. Acting like a teacher.
Little children jumping from here to there.
ABC and 123, easy peasy, lemon squeezy.
Forget the shopping and the fun.

Me and my family now celebrating
My amazing, fantastic future is no more a whisper.

Hatun Soran
Rush Croft Sports College, London

My Dream Is . . .

I have a dream today
But something's in the way,
I'm stuck at home playing games,
For the next six weeks with a broken hand.

But I still dream today playing for West Ham
And winning the grand slam,
Winning the League, cups and games and getting to play,
Getting on the pitch and winning the match.

For this to come true it will need just me and you,
Life is a big fat lie that comes true,
This dream spreads on like a forest fire,
'Save, save, save,' say the commentators.

Bradley Postlethwaite (12)
Rush Croft Sports College, London

My Poem

The world is a frightening place
People afraid to walk out the door
With youth quickly ready to pounce like animals
With the dangerous weapons

This is where the government comes in
They need to give us money
To get our youth off the street
And to get them into social clubs

Everyone is happy and delightful
No fighting, no war
No pain or suffering
People allowed to not live in fear.

Now that peace is among us all
There won't be any more violent duels.

Chris Norey
Rush Croft Sports College, London

I Have A Dream

In my curious dreams I soar above the sky
My head full of hopes and dreams, even though some of my hopes die.
I try . . .
All my bad dreams, they make me cry,
I promise to myself I'll never lie.
I try . . .
In my dreams I am alone, with no ally
Sometimes I wonder why?
And then I sigh . . .
I have a dream that the world will be in peace,
I pray to God to end it, I say please.
All of us have dreams, we can succeed
If we believe.

Keanu Adorable (12)
Salesian College, Battersea

People Of The World

People of the world less fortunate than us,
People of the world who need our trust,
People of the world who need our help,
People of the world who scream and yelp.

It's not their fault they live this way,
So they wait and hope to live another day.
It's time for us to make a stand,
And let them know that we understand,
That diseases like malaria can cause real death,
It will make you think twice and take a deep breath.

People die within a click of a finger,
How long will it take before it will hit ya?
So donate to those who are in need,
To eliminate malaria for everyone to see
That these people of the world are like you and me.

They aren't so different, we're all the same,
The only thing different may be our names,
We need to help them 'cause they're in need,
So hear my message I deeply plead.
It's now or never, so take that chance,
So they can jump for joy and laugh and prance.

People of the world, no need to worry,
People of the world, we'll show that we're sorry,
People of the world wipe away your tears,
People of the world we're here to stop your fears.

If I can make a change,
Then so can you.
If I can help the people in need,
Then you can help too.

Oke Omoniyi (12)
Salesian College, Battersea

I Have A Dream

I have a dream to one day let myself go,
Close my eyes and fly with wings,
Suppressing agitation inside them
Without a painful sensation,
Excruciation or agony
To look down as I used to look up at the sky every day.

Every second that has passed,
Dreams that have crashed may pass.

The infested feeling defiling your pain,
Suspended for life.

A feather falling from the sky,
Precipitating slowly,
Moving with defining attention,
Seeking its meaning of end and beginning.

What is the purpose for this dream
Seeking its true meaning?
Every feather that falls represents
A desire of each dream and what they mean.

The next second your eyes open,
It's not there,
Forcing you to leave it all behind,
Making a falling feather reach the end.
When it touches the floor there's no hesitation.

What matters is not giving up,
The tears of denial - let go
Don't reach the end of the line like a feather
Falling from the sky.

Dani Sherjeel (12)
Salesian College, Battersea

I Have A Dream

I had a dream of floating about
And dreaming of swimming like a trout.
I had no idea why the dream was so vivid,
Yet it flies about in my head.
It glides along my imagination!

I thought I was the only one,
The only soul that could understand,
But my dreams won't come down.
They die.

And I'll raise my dream up,
I won't let it die.

I had no idea what was going on,
I thought I was the only one.
This is the day that my dream will come true,
To wake up and there will be peace on Earth.

My dream is raising up,
The peace is coming.

Yet survive I do not know,
The wars should stop right now.

I just had to sway away . . .

My only dream. I am not alone.
All those dreamers come along.
We will join together and be as one
And there will be
Peace on Earth.

Sam Kotovas (11)
Salesian College, Battersea

I Have A Dream

One night I was in my bedroom
Looking in the sky,
Sitting there, watching the moon,
It was so bright,
Then I dreamed I had a girlfriend
And we were in the spotlight.

I went into my bed,
I had dreams in my head.
I was a Premier League footballer
And I was a lot taller.
My brother called me a baler!
Then I said to my dream girlfriend
After the match,
'I will call ya!'
I have a dream that I could play for teams
Wearing different colour schemes,
But you need to remember
That life doesn't come in dreams.

As my mum says,
You could play the lottery
But money doesn't grow on trees.
So if you have a dream,
Stick to it and you will see!

Trae Johnson (11)
Salesian College, Battersea

I Have A Dream

I have a dream to go to the moon . . .
I was scared when I approached the rocket.
I was thinking of running away and leaving this behind,
But I had to face my fears.

After I put on my suit
I was saying to myself that I can do this
And I can conquer this and be a man for once in my life.
I stepped on the platform and waited for my commander.
I saw him and knew it was time.
I spent most of my energy waiting for this terrible thing
In my life.
I took my seat.
My commander said, 'Why are you shaking, soldier?
Don't be scared. There's nothing to be scared about.
If we die, we die with honour in our names.'
We counted down from 10, 9, 8, 7, 6, 5, 4, 3, 2, 1 blast off!
It was terrifying, like my face was peeling off
As we went higher and higher.
I wanted out from this hell hole.
Then finally it stopped going high
And started to float into deeper space.
That's my dream and one day it might happen,
One day . . .

Sofiane Rincon (12)
Salesian College, Battersea

I Have A Dream

I have a dream
Of many ambitions
I have a dream
Of many missions

I dream I'm on stage in a West End production
Trapped in a cage
In a show called 'Abduction'

I dream I'm this adventurer
Travelling in the future
With one companion running from Mudwrenchers
Running riot on the planet Fluchure

I dream I'm at my dream job
Working in Rye
With no angry mobs
Cos they've all said bye-bye

My dreams are wild
But I believe in them
My visions are mild
In years of ten

I have a dream.

Josh Clark (12)
Salesian College, Battersea

Justice

Justice and unity are what we need.
We mustn't live a life of strife,
And not a life by a gun or a knife.

Live life to the fullest and don't get involved in crime,
Because I'm sure you wouldn't want to pay in jail doing time.
Everyone I know wants there to be harmony and peace,
So please be nice and sweet to everyone you see.

Never give up hope,
Just like the Pope . . . doesn't!
Give everyone a smile, it doesn't cost a thing.
Be kind, be loving and don't ever be smug.
If you see an old lady wanting some help,
Don't ignore her, go over and give her a hand.

If you see an elderly man who has dropped a penny,
Bend over and pick it up and he may say,
'You can have it young man, now run along sport.'

If everyone does what I ask today,
Then the world will be like a ball of play.
Be nice and sweet and never give up
And you will realise that the world has turned great!

Terrel Douglas (13)
Salesian College, Battersea

I Have A Dream

I have a dream that
No one else does,
I have a dream that
No one else has.

I have a dream that
I will live up to.
I have a dream to
Go in the army and
Become part of
The military
Police.

I have a dream
That hardly
Anyone will like.
I have a dream
That everyone
Questions.
I have a dream.

Mack Taylor-Preston (12)
Salesian College, Battersea

I Have A Dream

I have a dream that we will unite,
We shall be in peace and stop this fight.
The children will play out together again,
We shall bond, talk and stop this black pain.

We shall sit where we want and share all our goods,
We shall talk to our neighbours in our neighbourhood.
We shall not always fight and be in peace,
We should be a community, we should at least.

So our targets these years are to be kind, not mean,
We must unite, I have a dream.

Jordan Dedieu (13)
Salesian College, Battersea

The Dream Of A Better World!

My dream is where I want to see no poverty,
No crime that hurts people,
I want to see people saying hello to each other,
I want to see the place with
No drugs,
No guns,
No war,
No racism,
When I wake up I want to see
A peaceful place,
With no pollution,
Not a miserable, dull place
Because of bullies or bosses,
I want it so
There are no heavy crosses,
This is my dream, help me
To make it come true.

Edward Caunca (13)
Salesian College, Battersea

I Have A Dream

I have a dream that the world will be a better place
Where kids will play, no matter what the race
Where nobody is on anyone's case
And people don't laugh in other people's faces
The wars will end with a great bit hug
The streets will be clear of those bad thugs
Where the world will be free of all the drugs
Where we won't treat people like little bugs
Schools will not be filled with bullies
And people can share clothes when it turns out chilly
This is my dream that I have for the world
One day I pray it might come true.

Moses Adewale-Duckrell (12)
Salesian College, Battersea

I Have A Dream

My dream is . . .
My dream is a world without weapons
A world without someone dying
Without someone getting blamed for someone's death
A world without weapons would be Heaven

Julian Knight, 16
Police found Julian Knight bleeding from a knife wound to the neck
An ambulance took him to Elizabeth hospital
Doctors tried to save his life, but he died at 2.29pm

Would you be able to live with yourself
Knowing that you killed someone's son?

I know that I wouldn't be able to

Like the great Dr Martin Luther King
I have a dream
My dream is for weapons to be no more.

Sean Maposa (13)
Salesian College, Battersea

I Am Life

Life is everywhere
It is in you now and forever it shall stay
Life is the wind blowing sideways
Life is the winter and the summer
I am Life, you are Life, we are Life
I love Life and Life loves me
Life and I play beneath the midnight sun
Life and I play beneath the morning moon
Life kisses me goodnight and greets me with a smile
Life is sad and it is lonely
Life is evil and Life is blunt
Life is a true friend and never lies
I am Life, you are Life, we are Life.

John Bangui (13)
Salesian College, Battersea

I Believe In . . .

I believe
That everyone should be treated equally
I believe
That no one should be left out
I believe
That everyone should be given a chance
I believe
That everyone can play a part to change the world
I believe
That everyone can help someone else
I believe

I believe
That you can do something in an instant
That will give you a head start in life
I believe
Sometimes there is no explanation
I believe
Money cannot buy people's affection
I believe
You do not know what you have got until it is gone
I believe
I believe in second chances
I believe that life is as good as it gets

It's OK to believe in yourself.

Shannon Buckthorpe
Strathmore Centre, Twickenham

I Believe In Family

What is family?
Family is love
Family is special
Family helps you through troubled times
When things don't go right
Family will be there, there for you

Family is home
My home is my family
My home is where I feel safe
Safe from the trouble outside
Outside is cold but inside it's warm with my family

My family cares for me
My family are my friends
My family are always there to support me
My family guides me through life
They show me what is right and what is wrong
They comfort me through troubled times
My family is my most precious possession

I believe that everyone deserves a family
A family like mine
A family to keep you safe and warm
Families make the world a better place to be
I believe in family.

Connor Reddings
Strathmore Centre, Twickenham

Friends

Ingredients:
100g of love
100g of laughter
A pinch of fun
A gram of care
100% of trust
The most important ingredient is 100% friendship

Method:
Put the 100g of love into a bowl
Then add the 100g of laughter into the same bowl
Mix the love and laughter and add a pinch of fun to bring out the friendship
Then add a gram of care into the mixture
Then put the mixture into a baking tray and put it into the oven. Let it bake for 30 minutes at gas 250°C.
When it's done, add on top 100% trust and 100% friendship
Then put in oven for 5 minutes
And there you have a really good, real friend that you can count on and trust!

Andrea De Ville
Strathmore Centre, Twickenham

I Have A Dream

I have a dream to stop global warming,
I have a dream to keep nature soaring.
These little dreams in my mind
Are a whole new world for us to find.
I have a dream for no more wars,
I have a dream for new open doors.
These doors will open oh so wide,
To let peace and sunshine hit the skies.
All of these things we are able to do,
If we have our mind wide open, me and you.

Georgia Totten (12)
The Hemel Hempstead School, Hemel Hempstead

My Future

My mum and dad often say,
'What job will you perform someday?'
I sort of have a plan, or two,
Of things that I would like to do.
I get confused and change you see,
As lots of jobs appeal to me
And although I cannot say as yet,
I would dearly love to be a vet.
I would care for creatures, big and small,
Because I've always loved them all.
I even love those which crawl or slither
(but great big spiders make me quiver!)
Alternatively, I would like to do
Research on animals found in a zoo.
On the African savannah or American plains,
Proving our wildlife have good looks and brains.
I would discover vaccines and kill disease,
To ensure these rare animals never cease.
To make our planet a wonderful place,
This would put a smile on my face
But then again, I love my sports,
And I would like to be a star (of sorts),
In hockey or netball - I wouldn't mind either,
And to get paid for it wouldn't be bad - neither!
Be on TV, in the Olympic games,
And be remembered in their Hall of Fame.
Lots of medals, that would be funny
And like some footballers - plenty of money!
I'm so confused - what shall I do?
Work hard at school and learn things new!
Get my GCSEs and A levels, more,
And go to uni for a year - or four!
Maybe I'll take a year out
To tour the world on a 'walk about'.
It all seems so far away -
I'll make my mind up another day!

Charlotte Bartlett (13)
The Hemel Hempstead School, Hemel Hempstead

I Have A Dream

When I lay down at night
And shut my eyes,
I see those images that haunt me.

When I lay down at night,
And try to fall asleep,
I can't escape those voices.

When I lay down at night
And cry until the morning,
I see you
And I see me
And I hate it,
I hate it.

I am who I am,
You are who you are.
This world is the future, past and present
And we aren't involved.

When I lay down at night
And cry myself to sleep,
I see the world and then I see us.
We are different races,
Different worlds,
Different universes apart.
Why?
Tell me why.

When I lay down at night
And two colours flash before me,
Black and white,
Heaven and Hell.
I remember the days when black and white
Were friends, not enemies,
Were in peace, not at war,
Were seen no different from one another.

Now I see hatred.
I see fear.
I see pain
And I see you.

I want to hold you close,
I want to hold you near,
But we know we can't be together.
So just hold me, dear.

When I lay down at night
And I see your white-as-snow skin,
And I see my dark, ebony hands,
I watch the colours burn together
And wish this nightmare would cease.
We can make it,
If we try, we can shut everyone out.
I just wish I could believe it.

When I lay down at night
And I wish an empty vortex would suck me into its
Never-ending darkness,
I see us.
Together.
Forever.
And ever.
And ever.
And ever.

Amy Theobald (12)
The Hemel Hempstead School, Hemel Hempstead

Quarrels And Wars Will Be No More

There are visions flying all around the world
About things that matter
About problems that need to be dealt with
But each person owns one of those visions
And the one belonging to me is that there will be no need for dreams
That the world will be united
That no nightmares will be dreamt
That the good dreams will become actions
And the actions will change the world

Wars happen across the planet
Starting with small disputes
Growing larger and turning into arguments
Violence starts
Other people get involved
It spreads until countries fight and kill
Extremes happen like involving children with war
Drugging them and forcing them into battle
They become useless, addicted people after the war
Discarded like a broken weapon
Terrorised and scarred, possibly for life
Cruel things like child soldiers happen everywhere
Like a fire of crisis burning through nations of good people
Racism, child cruelty, animal cruelty, bullying . . .
The list goes on as far as the eye can see
The world leaders try their best to guide the countries
However, without the cooperation of others, the schemes will fail

All war takes energy
And if we channel that energy towards good things
And lead it to jump that first hurdle
The world will start to get better and recover from the disease
                                          that has corrupted it

So once this task is completed
The planet's people will start the tedious journey towards
                                          world peace
And conquer environmental problems like global warming, until all
                                          problems are solved

So there will not be any need for dreams

Nothing that will be dreamt could be better than the world we
                                                                                   live in
Because the world will heal and be perfect
And the harmony between nature and the human race will
                                                                      live forever.

Mary Pattinson (12)
The Hemel Hempstead School, Hemel Hempstead

Dream Poem

Looking through my student's book,
My eyes fell upon some beautiful art.
So many dreams, I couldn't help but look,
I knew this girl had a certain spark.

The first little sketch was framed with lights,
A beauty in a long dress, flaunting an award.
Tears sparkling her face in joyous cry,
She gestured to the crowd as they worshipped and roared.

Second daydream that tattooed the page,
Was cradling a wounded soldier, gun in hand.
Panting heavily, tears of rage,
Blood and dust on their saintly uniform, the dusty land.

The next tableau on the paper in the corner,
Was a white-coated angel that had the responsibility of lives,
At the side of the wounded was a wife and mourner,
But little did she know due to the doctor, her husband
                                                                     would survive.

Then, in the centre of the page, the fourth picture lay,
A firefighter, unconscious girl in arms,
Masking her ash-covered face from rippling flames,
In the background, a melted smoke alarm.

Ten years later this girl succeeded,
To nurse wounds in the army,
Saving lives and rescuing the weak,
I knew this girl had a certain spark.

Paige Baah (13)
The Hemel Hempstead School, Hemel Hempstead

Young Musician Of The Year . . . Yeah Right!

'Eliza D!' the judge declares. I walk up to the stage.
I feel like flying, as a bird would, released from my cage.
Smiling as I've won, I've won, my clarinet in hand,
Young Musician of the Year? I just don't understand!
That girl with the oboe can glare all she likes, the others might
stand tall,
But I don't care; I know already, I've outflown them all.

Flute, piano, violin, saxophone and drums,
All shrink back, and so they should, as here the clarinet comes!
Beethoven cannot be beaten, but I'm about to try.
His music fills my head and bursts out, spinning to the sky.
I've worked so hard for all my life, through all the highs and lows,
I've gone up, I've gone down, just like arpeggios.

Musicians dance in their graves, the heavens have to shake,
They celebrate along with me, with treble clefs and cake!
They helped me more than most, with their long-forgotten pieces,
When I pour my heart into their work, my confidence increases.
So I play like a star into heavens unknown, and with every note
I bring,
I notice someone appreciates the words my music sings.

Whoever brings rational thoughts is asleep; all I can think is laaa.
It's better than trumpeting trumpets; it's better than
strumming guitars.
Oh, my world is perfect, such a musical place . . .
And then I wake up and I stare into space.
My dream has been broken, but I know in my heart,
That it can be a reality, my playing's an art!

Even though I'm not famous, not brilliant (sigh),
The music keeps playing, low and then high.
B scale, Bb, Chromatic, C,
F scale, F#, Chromatic, E,
I think (deep inside me), I know what I'll do,

I keep up my posture, then straight past me flies . . .
A beautiful song thrush, just perfect, thank you!
I know at that moment, after all my tries . . .
My dream is imagined, but is true, true, true.

Eliza Dickinson (12)
The Hemel Hempstead School, Hemel Hempstead

I Have A Dream

I have a dream
I want to be part of the RAF team
I want to fly like a bird
And sting like a bee
I want to soar high
Right up in the sky
I want to fly round the world
Taking it all in my stride
I want to fight for my team
I want to fight for my country
I want to fire the guns
And have a lot of fun!
I want to save people's lives
And keep peace in the world
I want to make the world safer
From all the bad things out there
I want to fly the big ones
The B52 and the Hercules
And if I'm lucky
I'll fly the Airbus and jumbo jets
I'll look after my crew
And my passengers too
Keeping them safe
In the sky above
As I soar high
Right up to the sky
I have a dream
And I will take it one day at a time.

Mark Baldwin (13)
The Hemel Hempstead School, Hemel Hempstead

A Dream Of Happiness

As my eyelids droop,
I slip away to my favourite place.

The mists begin to clear
And I know I've left behind my fear.
A meadow is where I am,
Full of glistening daisies and buttercups.
My golden hair blows gently in the breeze,
While all around are buzzing bees.
I can't take my eyes away,
As the scene merges into a seaside bay.

I lie upon the golden sand,
And sieve it through my suntanned hand.
The sun shines down towards the beach
And the sea lies like a sleeping puppy.
Behind me palm trees start to sway
And out at sea the dolphins play.
I close my eyes to feel the glow,
But before I know it, I'm in the snow.

I open my eyes to witness the view,
The first thing I notice is the sky's amazing blue.
I can see everything all around,
Over every peak and every mound.
All around is glistening white,
Not a speck of dirt in sight.
I'm skiing down with the wind in my face,
Then suddenly I'm in a warmer place.

I snuggle into a comfy chair,
The heat from a fire is everywhere.
It snaps and crackles and eats the wood,
It would probably get me if only it could.
Abruptly, the tranquillity comes to an end,
My dreams are shattered, beyond mend.
A series of buzzing fills my head
And I reach out my fingers to the edge of the bed.

Ellie Ward (12)
The Hemel Hempstead School, Hemel Hempstead

Hopes And Dreams

My hopes and dreams are big and small,
Either way I wouldn't mind at all,
What I do or how far I go,
To find out more, keep on reading.

In the start of my life I didn't know what I wanted to do.
My sister started horse riding and that became her hobby,
Though I never seemed to know what I enjoyed,
Even though different things I did enjoy, I still wouldn't know.

After a couple of years my sister got a horse,
Though I was never interested in such a smelly hobby as that,
I one day met a girl who had what I needed to get into the horsey side of things!
She helped me build my confidence around horses.

Before I knew it, I was in the saddle myself.
She was always there, helping me get further along the line.
I thought she was great and hoped we would become closer friends.
We did and I'm still riding, though getting better each time,
Thanks to that girl who helped me.

I loved playing with Mum's make-up,
I would smudge it across my face though I would look like a clown,
We would end up scrubbing it off,
Because it got everywhere, even in my ears!

As I got older I took more interest in my appearance and wanted to be with the fashion.
I would play with my hair all day long, styling it in different ways,
Constantly worrying that my skirt was too long or my knee-highs were at my ankles.
That's what made my mind up, that I wanted to be a beautician.

I'm proud of myself in every kind of way,
That I built up that confidence and got in the saddle,
And took care of my looks.
Either way, I see what I want to be when I'm older,
A better horse rider and beautician.

Daisy
The Hemel Hempstead School, Hemel Hempstead

Global Warming

I see black, just black,
Nothing else, just black,
Everything's empty,
There's nothing to see.

*Splish, splash, splosh,
Boing, bing, bang,
Whoosh, wash, wish.*

Suddenly, I land,
There's nothing but sand,
Strange sand, just plain,
Everywhere's the same.

*Splish, splash, splosh,
Boing, bing, bang,
Whoosh, wash, wish.*

No houses, no trees,
No buildings, no bees,
Only sand, black sand,
Everything's bland.

*Splish, splash, splosh,
Boing, bing, bang,
Whoosh, wash, wish.*

All of a sudden,
Everything turns black,
I am petrified,
I get all muddled
(As you can see.)

*Splish, splash, splosh,
Boing, bing, bang,
Whoosh, wash, wish.*

Reduce
    Reuse
        Recycle!

Grace Masters (12)
The Hemel Hempstead School, Hemel Hempstead

To Visit The Titanic

I have many ambitions, but one stands out from the rest,
The others I can do anytime, so this one, for my future, is best.
My hope for later in life lies on the ocean floor,
It's such a sorry sight, it will make your heart weep to the core.
For this is the Titanic, the once thought unsinkable ship,
It was hit sidelong by an iceberg, a tearing noise, a gigantic rip.
On the 14th of April 1912, it sank beneath the waves,
It sent 1,517 people to their watery graves.
Now it lies half buried, covered by seaweed,
For the ship was going far too fast, travelling at maximum speed.

I would like to see this wreck and pay it my respects,
And think of all the people, of all the lost objects.
I would like to go down in a submarine
And watch through the window and look at the view screen.
It would be fascinating to see this grand old ship,
To ponder over what it looked like, before its icy dip.
It would be amazing to think I had visited
And to think of it, all damaged and rusted.
When I went down there, I would time two hours,
To see how long it took the sea to devour.

We would send the cameras down, to explore the different rooms,
I would see the Turkish baths, the kitchens and the bedrooms.
I would explore 1st class, 2nd class and 3rd class too,
I would see restaurants and cafes and where the ladies got
their hairdos.
The grand staircase and the ballrooms as well,
The writing rooms, where passengers wrote with quills and inkwells.
That is what I fancy doing when I am older,
To see all the funnels and all the ruined glamour.
To visit the Titanic, halfway to America,
It's certainly much better than watching documentaries,
sitting on the sofa.

Jessica Miller (13)
The Hemel Hempstead School, Hemel Hempstead

I Have A Dream

I have a dream
It is for the team
I hope that best
Will pass the test
Face the challenge
Will not take revenge
My smile will beam
I have a dream

Well-paid career
A family I will rear
Sometimes bad it may seem
I have a dream

With an upholstered house
And with an idyllic spouse
My eyes will gleam
I have a dream

Will keep them from starvation
And give respect to my nation
To help them in all life
I will cross the stream
I have a dream

Will protect my children when they cry
Love them dearly until I die
Help stop the fear when others scream
I have a dream

Get through the financial jobs
Complete the bits and bobs
Watch the footie on Sky
We will not win the World Cup again, I tell no lie
I have a dream.

George Brooks (13)
The Hemel Hempstead School, Hemel Hempstead

I Can . . .

Compete for my school team,
Win a penalty,
Captain a victory;
Earn a medal,
Play goal attack.
Perform for a club,
Score a goal.
Receive the centre pass,
Win a game.
Be selected for county,
Train really hard.
Be awarded a compliment,
Attempt the bleep test.
Pass it hard,
Be a team player.
Hold my space,
Outrun my opponent.
Contest for a place,
Get spotted for England.
Be a reserve,
Intercept a pass.
Play in the test series,
Continuously excel.
Become a regular,
Inspire my team.
Power to victory,
Be undefeated.
Be unstoppable,
Prove them right,
Prove them wrong.

Be like Pamela Cookey.

Francesca Quinn (12)
The Hemel Hempstead School, Hemel Hempstead

In My Dreams . . .

In my dreams . . .
Everything green,
Recycling,
Bicycling.
Rivers clean,
Polished sheen.
Forests intact,
It's a fact.
The world will survive
And we'll be alive.

In my dreams . . .
Dividing the cream.
Money to share,
Everything fair.
No more poor
Or spending on war.
Too much greed,
Not meeting the need.
The world will be nice,
Without avarice.

In my dreams . . .
People are keen
To be kind
And to find
New friends
And make amends.
For racism
Criticism.
The world a better place
When we share the same space.

Ben Johnson (13)
The Hemel Hempstead School, Hemel Hempstead

Do You Have Hopes And Dreams?

It's once in a lifetime that you have the dreams,
To stay on the right lines and strong at the seams.
If you take that advantage, then you'll go far,
Your dreams will come true and you'll be a big star.
If you just believe, then you know what you'll be,
Everyone will tell you; just you wait and see.
Now you see the light at the end of the tunnel,
They'll flow into one as if in a funnel.
Now you have the foundations to start anew,
When you've lived it before, you'll know what to do.

I dream that I can be many greater things,
To sing as a proven professional sings.
If I had one chance to show what I could do,
Then that chance would prove what I already knew,
That I had the strength and the confidence to try,
At that moment, my dreams would be high in the sky.
When things go right, you can go all the way,
You can do what you want as long as you stay.
Whatever you want to aspire to be,
You'll do what you want to a certain degree.

If you go far, you'll have many memories,
No could have, would have, should have or might have beens.
Please, never forget to make a decision,
Or lots of your thoughts will have a collision.
You do what you like, so why miss out on this?
You make a decision; your life will be bliss.
Don't hold back and hide away in the darkness,
If you don't, your life will be full of starkness.
So please, just follow all your hopes and your dreams,
To stay on the right lines and strong at the seams.

Jodie Hardcastle (13)
The Hemel Hempstead School, Hemel Hempstead

My Dreams

My hopes and dreams,
So it seems,
To be dictator of the Earth,
Now that's something of worth.

I'd like to view world peace, not world war,
No fighting, shooting, stabbing or gore,
A total elimination of world religion
And the execution of every annoying pigeon!

A main aspect is to give money to the poor,
More than enough to get them off the floor,
Stunningly swine flu will no longer be spread,
So I don't have nightmares in my bed.

I wish to have a special ability,
Like flying, fire or enhanced agility,
So I can protect the world from the sinful
And use each and every one of them as my experimental tool.

In 50 years' time I wish to see lasers,
Along with many anti-blunt razors,
And ships which can soar into the sky,
With many restaurants onboard which serve Thai.

I'd love to see comedy on stage every day,
Perhaps one time I could make a play,
That makes people snort and giggle
And I'll be a famous figure.

I also wish to have an amazing six-pack,
One which makes many women attack,
I want to have control over everything,
And have the strength and courage of a king.

Chris Andric (13)
The Hemel Hempstead School, Hemel Hempstead

I Have A Dream

When I grow up,
I want to be a presenter,
Drive convertibles,
Have nice stage clothes.

When I grow up,
I'd like to travel the world,
Buy a puppy,
Help lots of charities.

When I grow up,
I'd like to be on TV,
Living my dream,
Helping my family.

When I grow up,
Healthy and clean,
Raking it in,
Columns in magazines.

But I have to be careful what I say,
Or the press might hate me.
The public might hate me,
My friends might hate me.

Careful what I do,
Because the police might get me.
The important people might sue me,
My mum and dad wouldn't be pleased.

When I grow up,
I'd like to be a presenter,
Doing my family proud
And making my friends happy.

Jade Gardiner (12)
The Hemel Hempstead School, Hemel Hempstead

I Have A Dream

I have a dream, it's something to scream
In the future I can see dancing to the coolest beat
Hip hop dancing on a stage in the West End
Clapping and cheering, screaming to me
It is all a girl needs, going to see the Queen
Performing to Her Majesty

Dancing with a cheesy grin on my silly face
Grey trackie bottoms and a lime-green top
Wahay!
Stomping, clapping, sliding, grooving
That's the way you move it
Pop it, lock it, polka dot it
These are dance moves, yay!
Skipping and no tripping I make
Making my way up to centre stage
One slow, deep breath
Then start dancing
Shaking it from my head to my toes
The judges sit back and whistle
Their eyes draw right in to mine

My dream was right and at the exact time
As Simon Cowell said my name
I thought it was a silly game
The crowd went wild
My dream was through
I ended on a great move.

Victoria Bennett (11)
The Hemel Hempstead School, Hemel Hempstead

I Have A Dream

I have a dream of flying high,
So very high up in the sky.
The sky is blue, there are no clouds,
I am feeling so happy and proud.

The land below me is so green,
Shining grass that is squeaky clean.
Other fields are brown and yellow,
No one can hear me there, even if I bellow.

It is near the end of my exciting ride,
Then I walk off, showing my pride.
The hot sun rays beam down on me,
As I hear someone say, 'Where is he?'

When I look up to see the sun,
It blinds me like a shot from a gun.
People greet me as they walk past,
I wish this day would always last.

I walk to the beach on sand that is hot,
The birds in the sky look like little white dots.
The sea is cold, the tide comes in and out,
As I watch little children, running all about.

I sit on the beach and watch the sun go down,
Beautiful colours like on a ball gown.
It is the end of my journey, I have to go home,
To a wonderful place, where I will never be alone.

Lauren Stone (12)
The Hemel Hempstead School, Hemel Hempstead

I Have A Dream

'Everyone was screaming,
But he wasn't near me!
I want to be free!'
I hear you plea
'Not locked away without a key.'
This is what the interview sounded like.
'Please calm down now, Mike,
You're going to trial,'
A policeman said.
'It wasn't my fault that he's dead!'

At the trial I laid down my case
'Now his steps we must retrace.
There were fingerprints that were not his
But belonged to his wife, Liz.'
Everyone's face dropped in shock.
'And now that door you must unlock.
Go find his wife!
It's really her that used that knife!'

I want the world to be free from harm
And everyone to stand arm in arm.
I want the bad ones locked away
And the good ones to have a clear pathway.
Please help me, we'll work as a team
To achieve our lifelong dream.

Kathryn Tyne (13)
The Hemel Hempstead School, Hemel Hempstead

The Dream

When I am grown,
With my seeds mostly sown,
I dream of fame,
Though you may think it's lame,

I dream to win an Oscar,
Or even a Brit,
And then somehow my path will be lit,

I wouldn't preach,
As I made my speech,

'I'd like to thank,
My mum and dad,
The friends I have
And the people along the way,'

I have my award in my hand,
And I lead towards the lonely stand,
Please God, keep me steady,
Don't let me end up like my teddy,
And . . .

'Sophia, why are you lying down?
Don't make me frown.'

So it turned out it was only a dream,
If it comes true remains to be seen.

Sophia Amamou
The Hemel Hempstead School, Hemel Hempstead

My Dream World

In my dreams I see a
Foreign land where everyone is at peace.
There are no wars or deadly diseases
And everyone is at ease.

In this distant, magical land
Where no one cries, or ever suffers
There is a beautiful, unpolluted sky
That swoops above me, towering high!

It is the most amazing startling blue
And as I look up at it my heart fills with joy,
Then the wind blows a soft, gentle sigh
And I feel I could lift off the ground and fly!

I look all around and all I can see is
A swarm of smiling people beaming up at me
Their grinning teeth as perfect as pearls
And their luscious long locks in beautiful curls.

Then my eyes meet a wondrous sight
For an enchanting old oak tree dances in the wind
And a few stray leaves pirouette to the ground
Wonderfully whirling around and around.

This perfectly perfect world that I adore
Is my dream of our world, our future, and for evermore.

Jemma Whitbourn (12)
The Hemel Hempstead School, Hemel Hempstead

Dogs!

In the future I can see,
Many dogs cuddling me.
As I hold their paws so high,
I do not wish that they can die.
Black, brown, golden or white,
To wash their coats I have to fight.
Afterwards they're so dry and sweet,
So I give them all a tasty treat.
As my dogs go on many walks,
I stop by my friend's and have talks.
When we get home we are cold and chilly,
I have to check on my new dog, Billy.
I feed my dogs nutritious food
And I give them more when I'm in a good mood.
Afterwards they have a drink,
Fresh from the brand new sink.
I settle them down in a cosy spot,
Making sure they don't knock my pot.
As they gently fall asleep,
I say goodnight with a little weep.
I have such wonderful dogs I know,
As cute and cuddly as white snow.
I wish they could last forever and ever,
I know I can't because I'm not clever.

Lucy Church (11)
The Hemel Hempstead School, Hemel Hempstead

I Have A Dream

I have a dream,
I have a hope,
A target for the future.

An officer in the army?
To own my own restaurant?
An actor in a film?

To serve my country,
To be successful,
To play my part.

Work hard at school,
Do well in exams,
Go to university.

Will it make me proud?
Will it make me happy?
Will it make me rich?

Will one of my dreams come true?
Will one of my dreams become real?
Will one of my dreams change my life?

I have a dream,
I have a hope,
A target for the future.

Adam Nayler (13)
The Hemel Hempstead School, Hemel Hempstead

I Have A Dream

I have a dream in the night,
A big and scary, massive fright,
I have a dream in the night,
Weird and wonderful, joyous and bright.
I have a dream in the night,
An adventurous, monstrous, big old fight.
I have a dream in the night,
A happy, joyous, wonderful, awesome sight.
It is a man who makes the world a better place,
Keeps us joined as one
And a man who keeps us happy
And our friends beside us,
So don't be scared to be alive.

I have a dream and he is there,
Looking better than ever with his long, grey hair.
He is not a real man,
He is not a real being,
But he's the one that keeps me going.
His name I'm not sure of
And his clothes are really strange
And if you see him too,
I'm glad that he found you
Because he's the one who inspires me.

George O'Dell (12)
The Hemel Hempstead School, Hemel Hempstead

When I . . .

When I grow up,
I know what I want,
I know who I want to be.
When I grow up,
I want to see the world,
Drive nice cars,
I want to be remembered.
When I grow up,
I want a house,
A villa in the Med.
When I grow up,
The world would've changed
And I will be living my dream
And so it would seem,
That the endless list shall go on
And I will be remembered,
The day that I die,
I'll fly to Heaven
At half-past eleven,
But you will never forget me,
The day that I die,
A famous princess saying
Goodbye.

Zoë Dennis (13)
The Hemel Hempstead School, Hemel Hempstead

My Dreams Flow Like An Ocean

My dreams flow like an ocean,
Loud and proud and ready to be shared.
I dream of no wars, no worries,
Just to be at peace with my mind and others.

But when someone in the world comes so near to the truth,
People blow them away like leaves in the wind.
Why? I think, *why stop someone who is so close?*
And so the world carries on, fighting, worrying, hurting.

My dreams flow like an ocean,
But at the moment the world seems like it never was,
Something happens, then someone reacts,
And the world appears to sink in my hands.

I dream of no more hate, but happiness in its place,
Where everybody is content,
With no more death and no more fate,
But to be so happy would be great!

I want to scream like I've never screamed before,
To be heard just as a trumpeting elephant would,
But every time I open my mouth,
The world just ignores me, like I was never there.

Tessa Wilson (12)
The Hemel Hempstead School, Hemel Hempstead

I Have A Dream

I have a dream,
That this world can be peaceful,
With no wars or fights,
No vandalism or worrying.

So when people are asleep in their beds,
They don't need to worry,
They don't need to be scared.
For what is out there
May be a peaceful world.

No need to hurt people,
No need to kill,
Just to be together,
To be friends with one another,
To be kind to your sister and brother,
To be kind to your mother and father.

I have a dream,
That this world can be peaceful,
With no wars or fights,
No vandalism or worrying.

This dream could be true.

Olivia Pinnock (12)
The Hemel Hempstead School, Hemel Hempstead

My Dreams At Night

In the future I wish to be
A science teacher with experiments to see
Whizz, bang, sparks galore
Chemicals into the pot I'd pour

I dreamed a dream that the future will be
A better place for you and me
No knives, no crime, just good people
And the bell ringing loudly on the steeple

In the future the world shall be
No wars, no poverty, no stinging bees
We will not have to have charities, it'll all be fine
And Mount Everest I will climb

In the future I wish to be
A lead in the West End, Oliver maybe
Or a professional singer would do nicely
But with my voice it wouldn't be likely!

So there you are
There are my dreams
The future just seems so close . . .
It seems.

Philippa Gobby (13)
The Hemel Hempstead School, Hemel Hempstead

I Have A Dream For Football

I have a dream that I could play for Arsenal,
I could play for the England team,
And be the captain.

I have a dream that I could meet my hero, Peter Shilton,
And have the best goalie gloves,
I wish I had the best football boots.

I have a dream that I am everybody's favourite,
And all the girls love me,
I wish I never gave up on the team.

I have a dream that I could be the funniest on the team,
And I could be the tallest.
When I am older I want to be like Brian Clough.

I have a dream when I grow up I could win the World Cup,
I wish I could win the Champions League with Arsenal,
Then go on to win the World Champions trophy.

I have a dream that when I grow up
I will be the best goalie in the world
And then die in the best stadium, Wembley.

Charlie Hoskins (12)
The Hemel Hempstead School, Hemel Hempstead

I Have A Dream

I have a dream,
That birds can fly,
Without being shot from the sky,
Down to Earth they'll never come,
Unless they're feeding their little ones.

I have a dream,
That deer can play,
Without being frightened away,
From hunters with awful guns,
That will kill their loving mums.

I have a dream,
That fish can race,
Without humans giving chase,
With their very scary net,
That brings those fish right out of the wet.

I have a dream,
A dream,
A dream.

Caitlin Filby (11)
The Hemel Hempstead School, Hemel Hempstead

I Have A Dream

I have a dream that one day poverty will be history
I have a dream that people will not be treated as objects
They will be treated as individuals with respect
I have a dream that no matter what people look like
Or what their skin colour is, we treat them equally.

I have a dream that I can achieve anything I want to
Do anything that I wish to do and successfully reach my goal
I have a dream that my dedication and determination
Will get me to where I want to be
I have a dream that I will believe in myself
And all of my family and friends will too.

I have a dream that in my future life I will be where I want to be
Doing what I want to do.

I have a dream that if you hold on
To what you've always wanted to do
You will get there in the end
And be the person that you've always wanted to be.

Charlotte Ballard
The Hemel Hempstead School, Hemel Hempstead

I Have A Dream

My hopes and aspirations are to be a game designer.

As a game tester in my 30s, I would test games from
Nintendogs on Nintendo DS to Guitar Hero on PS2.
I would test them to the limit, trying to find any faults
With the game which I could possibly point out for the
Designer of the specific game.
Later in my life, I would probably get bored with sitting
In a room constantly testing games, so I am going to
Become a race car driver when I am about 40 years old.
I would be racing with Brawn-Mercedes racing team's
Formula 1 car around the Laguna Seca raceway on one race.
My pit stop crew will be trained to perfection to do pit stops
And the equipment for undoing the wheel nuts
Will be cutting edge, making pit stops at least one second quicker.
This may make a difference between 1st place and 2nd place.
These dreams and aspirations may be quite far-fetched
But if I work hard I may be able to achieve them.

Chris Mann (13)
The Hemel Hempstead School, Hemel Hempstead

Dream

I'm not mean,
I'm just seen
And always followed around
By the senior management team.
I'm a human being,
And I'm clean,
I'm straight, not lean.
I'm 5'6 in height,
Or 5'7, maybe in-between,
Got long hair, very clean.
I hold it in, don't let off steam,
I don't have one - I am the dream!

Malouki Servis (14)
The Hemel Hempstead School, Hemel Hempstead

I Have A Dream

I have a dream
It's with the England football team
We will win the Olympic games
Whilst the others walk away in shame

I have a dream
I was inspired by Aaron Lennon
His speed, strength and determination
There will be one captain
Who goes out to win
He will take us to the gold
This is what we've been told

I have a dream
To have my hands wrapped round the cup
And hold my medal high, high up
We will achieve and succeed

I have a dream . . .

Conor Blake (13)
The Hemel Hempstead School, Hemel Hempstead

Living The Dream

When I grow up I'll become a writer,
Like JK Rowling or Roald Dahl.
Inspired by family and friends,
I will be living the dream,
Exploring the world, opening my mind,
Will give me a chance to find what's inside.
Escaping from reality, finding a new world,
Will be all I need to live the dream.
Inspiring others to live their dream,
Will be all that I need.
Young or old, short or tall,
Everyone should do what they want to do.
Each year that passes, the more my mind grows,
Learning from my mistakes, getting stronger every day.
Until the day I am living the dream,
I will always have a dream.

Megan McKenzie (13)
The Hemel Hempstead School, Hemel Hempstead

Dreams

I had some dreams,
Life isn't as bad as it seems.
You start to think
And then all of it starts to link.
Life doesn't have to be scary,
You can't rely on a fairy.
Once in a while you need to stand up for yourself
Because you know you deserve better health.
So if we join together,
In your life it could be better weather.
Dreams can make you understand,
Dreams can give you inspiration,
Dreams can give you the life you deserve.

Christie Jackson (11)
The Hemel Hempstead School, Hemel Hempstead

I Have A Dream

It was a dream,
Just an ordinary dream.

It started in the summer breeze,
People playing and swimming in the sun,
Determination on their faces,
Trying to please their beloved one,
Still alone,
As time goes by,
Watching all the fun,
Still no joy comes to me,
Cos I've lost my loving one.

I saw the kites flying high,
Wishing I was there,
Up to Heaven I want to go,
My family are waiting there.

Isabel & Morwenna Hooker
The Hemel Hempstead School, Hemel Hempstead

Love

Love, love, love shines like the sun in the sky
It brightens up everybody's day
But I may hear you ask, 'How and why?'
'How and why?' I may hear you say
It makes you wonder how love came to be
Makes you wonder how it happened to you
If it happens to you, will you ever see?
Even then, will you know what the future holds?
But let us hope it will be good
And stay that way, not succumbing to the cold
Probably just like we think it should
I love you so much, you are my whole world
You're the reason I wear my hair curled.

Holly Lamb (14)
The Hemel Hempstead School, Hemel Hempstead

My Sonnet

I have a dream to make a better world,
For the angry Earth to unite in love,
For claws of fury that bind us unfurl,
To form land tranquil as Heaven above.
I have a dream for starvation to end,
For a roof to fall above homeless heads,
For broken hearts and families to mend
And hapless souls to sleep sound in their beds.
I have a dream for children to live free,
For merciless child abuse to cease,
For blinded minds of abusers to see
That children have a right to live in peace.
We can create a greater human race,
My dream? To make the world a better place.

Jordan Kelly (14)
The Hemel Hempstead School, Hemel Hempstead

The Crime Fighter

I'm chasing you down the motorway,
In my high visibility car,
I'm a cop,
Stop!
You're breaking the law,
Don't take your life down this way.

The laws are there for everyone to keep,
So don't blast it down the road,
You think you're awesome but really you're not,
And remember the law's on my side.

This is what I want to be,
Fighting crime will be my job,
It's a dirty job but I'll do it well,
You won't be laughing when I've got the cell key.

Sam Turner (13)
Wyvern College, Laverstock

Dream Dimensions

Dreams are dimensions
Aside from this world
Daring but fun
People's lives they mould.

Some are good
Others are bad
Each one is rather different
Sometimes they relate to a fad.

The dimension is dark and sparkling
When someone nods off
Their brain lights up the world of dreams
And makes that gracious world shine.

Monsters are imagined
They come back, both big and small
Whatever you think up
It will come to play!

Things are imagined
Not long later and then they appear
Fun and terror can be brought
Dreams and nightmares are caused.

But soon light and dark looms
Night looms in our world
The dimension of dreams soon turns dark
And soon we are awake.

This causes dreams to . . . end!
But they come again the next night
And the next and so forth!
Soon the dream dimension will be back!

Harry Richardson (14)
Wyvern College, Laverstock

The Planet's Creatures

The animals came, they were all alone,
Then humans came and they picked up a bone.
The world was changing,
The planet was raging,
The apes began to stand,
They were upright on the land.
They caused no harm,
They could not even farm,
Their brains began to grow,
The Earth began to slow.
They picked up some tools
And began to make stools,
Then they started to hunt,
The animals felt the brunt!
They started to kill,
They thought it a thrill.
The animals were going,
But the humans were growing.
Extinction was coming
And the animals were running.
We still haven't learnt,
From what we have burnt
And it needs to be sorted
As things are distorted.
We need to sort out,
What we brought about.
This is number one -
It needs to be done.

Joshua Bartlett (14)
Wyvern College, Laverstock

Nameless Poem

A runway, an airport, a pilot
The bird has no worries
The fuel, the time, the place
The bird has no worries.

The open sky, the confined sky
The soaring freedom, the route restriction
Light as a feather, heavy as a train
Fast as a bird, but not like a plane.

No need to consider, the rest of the world
Only ever looking, for the next meal
Soaring and gliding for hours on end
Just going and going 'til food has been found.

Safety precautions, talks and checks
Food, drink, entertainment, comfort
Nothing is forgotten, at the passenger's expense
While all the executives count their wealth

I'd love to be a pilot
I'd love to be a bird
But a pilot is much better
He gets paid to do his wonderful job!

Ashley Turner (13)
Wyvern College, Laverstock

Roller Coaster

I have a dream I will create the world's best roller coaster,
Which everybody will love and
I'll donate the money I earn to charity.
I hope my roller coaster is a big hit,
I can't wait to ride my ride, it will be a blast to ride.
I dream the queue for my ride will be hours long.

Tom Hedges (12)
Wyvern College, Laverstock

My Dream

I have a dream that one day
Black and white children will play,
Hand in hand, they shall say,
Freedom is well on its way.

I have a dream that freedom
Will last for all the years to come,
War will be gone from our world,
To freedom's drum.

I dream that all will love who,
Children of Earth, every Jew.
Together sang, together grew,
Songs of freedom, all they knew.

Proclaimed Martin Luther King,
Songs of freedom let us sing.
Peace to Earth we shall bring,
From every mountain freedom ring.

I have a final dream where we breathe freedom like air,
Singing of freedom we will not care.
For freedom, like air, is there,
Universally, all will share.

Taylor Budgell (13)
Wyvern College, Laverstock

My Awesome Future

I have a dream to be a cop
I hope I end up on top
I want to stop crime
No matter what the time

Travel the world I'd love to do
To see Japan, Russia and Peru
I would go in my trusty boat
I would need a raincoat

I really want to jump out of a plane
I'm hopeful I won't feel any pain
I would need to be pushed out
I would definitely scream and shout

I would love to scuba dive
I hope I come out alive
I would love to see a shark
But not in the dark

If these happen it will complete my life
Especially with kids and a wife
Then I'd buy a dog or a cat
Then I'd be an old man with a pipe and a hat.

John Light (13)
Wyvern College, Laverstock

The Earth's Dream

Based on my beliefs and thoughts,
Creatures, humans of all sorts,

Everything destroyed by global warming,
When this happens the Earth will be forming.

We watch from above, new beings arrive,
We are stunned, as new people come to life.

Any theories are uncovered,
Many things are discovered.

These new people have equality,
Everything is as good as it can be.

The ice is back - right in place,
As long as we don't quarrel over our race!

The world is back with nothing wrong,
No earthquakes will sing their song.

If we stop our sins and cravings,
We can go back to discount savings!

No problems on this amazing planet,
This is how we should have run it!

Jacob Ashton (13)
Wyvern College, Laverstock

The Future's Bright

I had a dream . . .
Of a better future . . .
Of a brighter future . . .

For me!

I dreamt I had an Aston Martin DB9
I really think that would be fine
I thought I had a Porsche 911
I really think that would be heaven.

I dreamt I had a massive house
With lots of children and a mouse!
I wonder who will be my wife
And hope for certain it's for life!

I dreamt I had an awesome job
Earning more than average Bob
I dreamt I worked for Top Gear
And presented to people far and near.

The future's bright . . .
So that's alright!

Ross Keel (13)
Wyvern College, Laverstock

Beginning

An end has a start, a start has an end
But where's the beginning?

The sun sets in the west
And rises in the east
But what we all want is a world of peace

A world of love
Symbolised by the white dove

As the hungry wolf howls at the moon
Hoping and praying for doom and gloom

Children play in the street
As the wolf howls to the beat

He cries and sings
To rid the world of all the sins

But when will we win?
When will we sing?

So you've read my start and here's my end
Now you choose where it begins.

Joe Willicome (12)
Wyvern College, Laverstock

The World Has Dreams

I have a dream
To see the world and its people
To see the time when everyone is equal
To save the world from global warming

We have a dream
To see the largest diamond on this Earth
To have a million pounds in worth
To give everyone in the world a fair trial
And to see a new solar system

The world has a dream
To make the world a better place
To make every man free for their race
To save the world from starvation
And to cure every illness

I have a dream
To see the world
As a perfect world.

Dan Hyde (13)
Wyvern College, Laverstock

Cricket

I have a dream of cricket
Where I would keep wicket
I'd hit sixes galore
Even on the floor
And I will never nick it.

If I become a star
I will go very far
I will win the Ashes
With lots of smashes
Then buy a sports car!

Nick Hillier (14)
Wyvern College, Laverstock

To Be A Star

I have a dream,
My perfect dream,
To sing on stage,
To get engaged.

Have my face on a shoe,
Or maybe even on a boob.
I'd stand on the roof of my mansion,
Singing, rapping, raving and dancin'.

I hope this dream will come true,
To make me happy, even you.
To be as famous as the Queen,
I really hope this is the dream.

I hope to be in everyone's heart,
To be on top in the number one chart.
To have a butler running round for me,
This is the life I've wanted it to be.

Scott Hutcheon (13)
Wyvern College, Laverstock

The Unfortunate

I dream of riches, wealth and power,
But some people don't have a shower.
When I think of this,
I remember how lucky I am.
I want to help and give,
Then maybe some people can live.

I think about an easy life,
But someone may have lost their wife.
I think of famine and disease,
When I see people on their knees.
Sometimes I think about power over the elements,
When some people barely have settlements.

Ben Percy (13)
Wyvern College, Laverstock

A Dream Of Peace And Happiness

I once had a dream,
Where an unhappy man screamed,
To stop all war,
To end all gore.

I have a dream where all have a house,
With no one left sleeping out,
Where we all have a right to be free,
Where all are happy, he or she.

A dream where the sun shines above,
And all are peaceful like a dove.
Where all follow the law,
And there is no such word as gore.

I had a dream where all help each other,
Whether they're a child or a mother.
Then all of a sudden, the unhappy man smiled
And said, 'I hope it lasts for a while.'

Scott Quinn (12)
Wyvern College, Laverstock

War Is Hell

Ben is his name
And saving the world is his aim.
He's in the army, clean and fresh,
Everybody says he's the best.
He uses a sniper to give them pain,
To him it's just like one big game.
His friend has just died by one air strike,
He keeps looking up in the pitch-black night.
He lies awake at night thinking of his friend,
And also how this might be the end.
Morning comes then it's the same routine,
Killing, dying, crying, he doesn't think it's a game any more.

Ben Martin (12)
Wyvern College, Laverstock

A Greener Future

I have a vision to see no pollution
To see no more trees die in the future
This is the best possible conclusion
To build a big, healthy culture

To create a greener way to travel
To eliminate the big polluters
To see people walk on paths made from gravel
To get rid of all the big commuters

To see wildlife return to countrysides
To see animals populate more than ever
Maybe to take a walk on the wild side
It's not easy, it's not like pulling a lever

Now that was my vision
Now you try and do some revision
So you can make the world a better place.

Harry Dredge (12)
Wyvern College, Laverstock

A World Of Dreams

In a world where your reality dissolves,
In a world the planet never revolves,
A world where air is still as rock,
A world where time will never tock.

This dreamland I call another place,
The one where magic and creatures unfold,
It's somewhere in an empty space,
One where we will never grow old.

My dreams will never cease to leave,
No matter how much I try to retrieve,
An eternity in this peace and joy,
It's all in my mind, a treasured toy.

Nathan Sainsbury (14)
Wyvern College, Laverstock

Equal

They sit on the street all night and day
They have no job, they have no pay
They sleep on the street, cold and weak
The night is so very bleak
They try to find money to make ends meet
They try to find a tasty treat
Many have a Tesco trolley
If it rains they find a brolly
They sit with that friendly mouse
Oh, I bet he wishes he had a house
They carry things but haven't much
I wish they wouldn't touch
I bet you would like a nice big roast
But I wouldn't like to boast
Can't we all be fair, equal and kind?
I mean we all have a human mind.

Jonny Adair (12)
Wyvern College, Laverstock

Football Manager

I have a dream of being Manchester United's manager
That I will buy Messi and Kaka
That we will win 30 titles
That we will do the treble, reliving the famous moment in 1999
And that we will be the best in the world
But now to my personal life
I hope I will have a Bentley
That I will have a mansion in England and Spain
I will have a wife and children
And I wish this will not just be a dream.

Jack Biggins (12)
Wyvern College, Laverstock

A Perfect World

I look to the west and I look to the east,
Then I realise the world hasn't got a lot of peace,
As I think of poorer countries when I indulge in my feast.

Is there any need for racial abuse?
I haven't got any time for any excuse.

Tears shed from eyes of people in poorer countries,
Let's take the time for respect and send them munchies.

Some can be rich and some can be poor,
But there's always a place for one more.

So this is my dream,
Beamed to me by a man,
With a face,
Who lives in a heavenly place.

Macauley Njie (12)
Wyvern College, Laverstock

All I Want Is Peace

My dream is for the world to be at peace
And every public place to be healthy and clean.

I want this world to be racial discrimination free
And no comments that are taking the mick out of me.

Now the war has come to an end
No one ever decides to pretend.

As the war has ended, people are crying
All the soldiers stopped trying.

It is now coming to the end of my horrible dream
My life is becoming less free.

As we are all equal, there should be no abuse
And now it is time to say, 'ciao, ciao'.

Dylan Hall (12)
Wyvern College, Laverstock

Peace Is A Sight

Peace is a sight that crops up in my dreams
And where every man and child is free.
They are equal as it quite seems,
But as I look closer, they aren't like me.
As I sit and daydream in this class,
I wish that people would be at peace.
As I stare out of the double-glazed glass,
There is no peace to the west or the east.
As I walk down this quiet city street,
There is a fight going on down the road.
As I walk around to the city beat,
Then a big crash, two lorries, both heavy loads.
We all live under one bright sun that beams,
That's what everyone wants, I have a dream.

Kieran Winfield (12)
Wyvern College, Laverstock

Random Dreams

I have dreams every night,
In one, three snakes bite.
I'm in a desert, with two people next to me,
What a shame no one's helping me.
Then I'm in space, on Mars,
How random, there's my car.
I go to it and switch it on,
Suddenly, I'm at home playing the drums.
I look back and the three snakes are there,
Then I see my parents stand there and stare.
This is how random my dreams are,
The snakes, Mars and the car.
I've never ever finished a dream,
But I guess it just goes on till the next scary scream.

Robert Mills (12)
Wyvern College, Laverstock

I Have A Dream

I have a dream to be really wealthy
But in some cases people aren't healthy
I want to have an amazing sports car
So in this life I can really go far
I want to own an almighty big house
Just like the superhero, Danger Mouse
I want to have a very busy job
But I don't want to make an angry mob
I want to be in the battle of war
And in this war there's someone in the door
In this crummy wasteland there are dead men
And in this field is my good friend, Ken
So in this poem I am writing you
I give you a very, very fair do.

Anthony Sturges (13)
Wyvern College, Laverstock

Young Writers Information

We hope you have enjoyed reading this book - and that you will continue to enjoy it in the coming years.

If you like reading and writing poetry drop us a line, or give us a call, and we'll send you a free information pack.

Alternatively if you would like to order further copies of this book or any of our other titles, then please give us a call or log onto our website at www.youngwriters.co.uk

Young Writers Information
Remus House
Coltsfoot Drive
Peterborough
PE2 9JX
(01733) 890066